_RTS S_NT_ MÒNIC_

ART SITUACIONS

A_PROSPECTIVE_LOOK

Mauro_Cerqueira
Pepe_Cifuentes/flo6x8
Patricia_Dauder
Carla_Filipe
Nuria_Fuster
Santiago_Giralda
Jaime_de_la_Jara
Miki_Leal
Juan_López
Francesc_Ruiz

_RTS S_NT_ MÒNIC_

Edition
Ediciones Polígrafa
and Arts Santa Mònica

Distributors
Ediciones Polígrafa
Balmes 54, entlo. 2ª
08007 Barcelona
Tel.: +34 933 968 846
Fax: +34 934 672 172
info@edicionespoligrafa.com

Llibreries de la Generalitat
de Catalunya
www.gencat.cat/publicacions

ISBN
978-84-343-1310-1 Polígrafa
978-84-393-8833-3 ASM

Legal deposit
B-5.377-2012

Arts Santa Mònica
La Rambla, 7
08002 Barcelona
Tel.: +34 93 316 28 10
www.artssantamonica.cat

Ediciones Polígrafa
www.edicionespoligrafa.com

HONDA
www.hondaencasa.com

ART Situacions
www.artsituacions.com

GENERALITAT DE CATALUNYA
DEPARTMENT OF CULTURE

Councillor for Culture
Ferran Mascarell

General Secretary
Xavier Solà

Director General of Cultural
Promotion and Cooperation
Jordi Cabré

ARTS SANTA MÒNICA

Director
Vicenç Altaió

Arts Area
Manuel Guerrero

Administrative coordination
Conxita Oliver

General coordination
Fina Duran
Marta Garcia

Public relations
Alicia Gonzalez

Editions
Cinta Massip

Press and communication
Neus Purtí
Cristina Suau

Production and coordination
Lurdes Ibarz
Ester Martínez
Arantza Morlius

Technical Area
Xavier Roca
Eulàlia Garcia

Administrative office
Pep Xaus
Carles Ferry

Arts Santa Mònica gratefully acknowledges the support of the Corporació Catalana de Mitjans Audiovisuals, of *La Vanguardia*, *Vilaweb* and *Mau Mau* as collaborating media

HONDA
GREENS POWER PRODUCTS, S.L

Director General
Marcel Pascual

Director of ART Situacions
Pilar Forcada

EXHIBITION

Direction
Pilar Forcada

Experts Committee
Teresa Blanch
María de Corral
Yolanda Romero
Vicente Todolí

Scenographical design
Llamazares Pomés Arquitectura

Graphic design
Edicions de l'Eixample

Production
Jaume Rosell – Solucions Globals

Honda coordination
Sònia Manzano
Joan Ramon Vinyals

Arts Santa Mònica coordination
Ester Martínez

Installation
Marc Ases
Juan Carlos Escudero
David Garcia
Xesco Muñoz
Luis Bisbe
Juan de Dios Jarillo
Pere Jobal

Acknowledgements
Fundació Antoni Tàpies
Galeria Estrany-de la Mota
Galería Fúcares
Galeria Nuno Centeno
Galeria ProjecteSD

With the special collaboration of
Arcadi Calzada
Elvira Maluquer
Conxita Oliver
Violant Porcel

Arts Santa Mònica, Barcelona
From 9 February to 15 Abril 2012

BOOK

Texts
Teresa Blanch
Mauro Cerqueira
Pepe Cifuentes
María de Corral
Patricia Dauder
Carla Filipe
Pilar Forcada
Nuria Fuster
Santiago Giralda
Jaime de la Jara
Pedro de Llano
João Pinharanda
Arnau Puig
Yolanda Romero
Francesc Ruiz
José Julián Soánez
María José Solano Franco
Vicente Todolí
Ignacio Tovar

English translation
Traduït (traduit.cat)
with
Paul Martin
Tracy Byrne
Fiona Missett
Debbie Smirthwaite
Jon Selwyn

Editorial coordination
Joan Riambau

Graphic design
Saura-Torrente,
Edicions de l'Eixample

Production
Ediciones Polígrafa

Prepress
Estudi Polígrafa / Annel Biu

Printing
Nova Era Barcelona

Director of ART Situacions
Pilar Forcada

Experts Committee
Teresa Blanch
María de Corral
Yolanda Romero
Vicente Todolí

Table of contents

Art, knowledge, innovation, society

It is often said that the art of innovation, which derives from the avant-garde, opens up the vision of the future better than the art of representation, which underlies the present time. And the fact is that one of the traits of enlightened modernity, namely "a prospective look," is held to be a humanistic value: the capacity of observing and constructing hypotheses and predictions. It is significant that at a moment of uncertainty, of profound crisis and reformulation, a bold exhibition is presented with no other prime intention than to read, select and display the situation of emerging art and to do so with a selective wager in favour of the new generation.

The world of art, when it overcame its extreme formal, linguistic and social radicality in the wake of conceptual art, found itself reborn in a startling explosion in the late decades of the 20th century. Avant-garde art reached the general public in the same way as young people's art was received practically without distinction in regard to the classics. Contemporary art museums and centres were opened everywhere; all kinds of tendencies coexisted; the presence of the arts was a sign of progress in both private homes and companies; art collecting reached a fever pitch; the galleries grew, and an avalanche of young people trained to become students and teachers, like so many other producers of the multiple arts, from the functional arts of design to the creative visual and behavioural arts. And suddenly, what certain thinkers had warned about in regard to the long central peace and the goodness of post-modernity came to pass: the system that had won followers (sociabilisation) and accelerated growth imploded. The shift from material culture in the technoglobal society towards the knowledge society entered into crisis, the material culture being incapable of sustaining the so-called immaterial culture.

The Arts Santa Mònica Centre, which combines the present with the various verb tenses constructed by memory and innovation, and which manifests its alertness to mutations and changes, welcomes and collaborates, presents and promotes, one of the initiatives of patronage and collecting, that of Pilar Forcada and Marcel Pascual, who, starting out from a prestigious award dedicated to painting, have had the capacity to reformulate it and extend it to the diverse forms and manifestations in which today's art expresses itself – a vital contribution that reassumes the leadership of patronage with the participation of prominent specialists in teaching, curatorship, museology and management of art centres. Their vision – restless, passionate and teeming with experience of life and professional activity – has been translated, after several shared working sessions, into the configuration of a prospective map on artistic creativity in the Iberian Peninsula.

This effort has received the support of the professional team of Honda, the architects, the graphic designers and the co-editor of the catalogue, along with numerous gallery owners who are again promoting art from the viewpoint of the concerns of a period that is in deconstruction and construction, both inside and outside the systems of art and politics.

The artists presented here were born during the final throes of the dictatorships and were trained in a context of democracy and the full integration of Spain and Portugal into a Europe that embraced both the post-communist north and the post-fascist south. They are well-known figures in today's panorama of private and public art, and their work imbibes of the spirit of enlarging the social limits of art.

Vicenç Altaió
Director of Arts Santa Mònica

ART_Situacions, a_prospective_look

The system of values on which our society has long rested now finds itself in a period of total redefinition. Culture and art constitute an effective tool for honing our criteria, a path that may illuminate the uncertainty in which humanity finds itself immersed. It is this conviction that is the genesis of ART Situacions, an invitation that seeks to support emerging contemporary art.

From the Middle Ages to the present day, private initiative has constantly fostered artistic creation. We could draw a line from the Medici family, the driving force behind the Renaissance, to Heiner Friedrich and Philippa de Menil, the promoters of the Dia Art Foundation, who encouraged the development of minimal art, to cite just two illustrious examples that are widely separated in time. This proposal is a new step in stimulating private initiatives, foundations and collectors, along with all art lovers, with whom we are delighted to associate ourselves.

Being well aware of the scarcity of opportunities for the youngest sector of present-day art, ART Situacions aims to promote its dissemination and to bring it to a broader public. It does not seek to reflect the tastes of the collectors themselves, nor to promote any particular artistic theme or discipline, but rather to constitute a prospective look.

In this edition we have the honour of receiving the collaboration of Teresa Blanch, María de Corral, Yolanda Romero and Vicente Todolí, specialists of national and international prestige who have jointly selected ten artists to create an incisive panoramic vision of the youngest generations in Spain and Portugal.

Without doubt, this is an evocative group of creators with international projection, who are exhibiting undisplayed works made from various media, from paint and the object to video or performance action. A stimulating landscape of great polyhedric capacity, united by a firm desire to rethink the relationship of humanity with its environment.

For us, it is a great satisfaction to give our economic support both to Spanish culture and the participating artists, along with Arts Santa Mònica and the Generalitat de Catalunya, with the shared desire to energise the artistic sphere. I would also like to express our gratitude to all the people of the cultural world who, with their unconditional support, have made it possible to consolidate the invitation announcement.

Pilar Forcada
Director of ART Situacions

Mauro Cerqueira

Mauro Cerqueira strikes a difficult, fragile balance in his sculptural works, combining what seem to be the remains of a shipwreck, elements found which he uses to construct works of a rare poetry. Through these he alludes, on the one hand, to movements such as constructivism or Arte Povera and, on the other, to an aesthetic that focuses on discovering what has been rejected/abandoned, imbuing everything with a highly personal perspective where his own body often acts as a reference, also leading him to explore the disciplines of video and performance.

Vicente Todolí

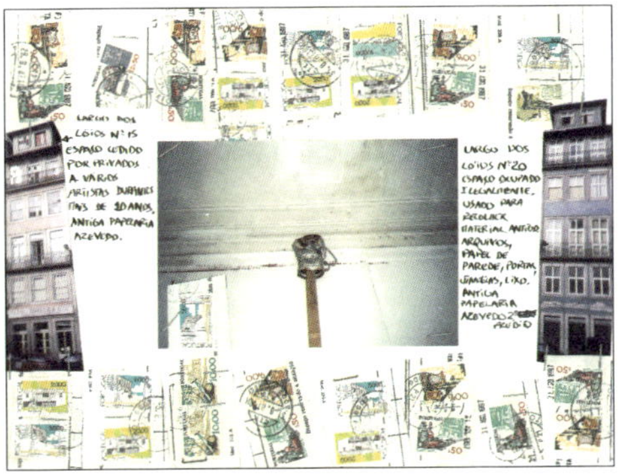

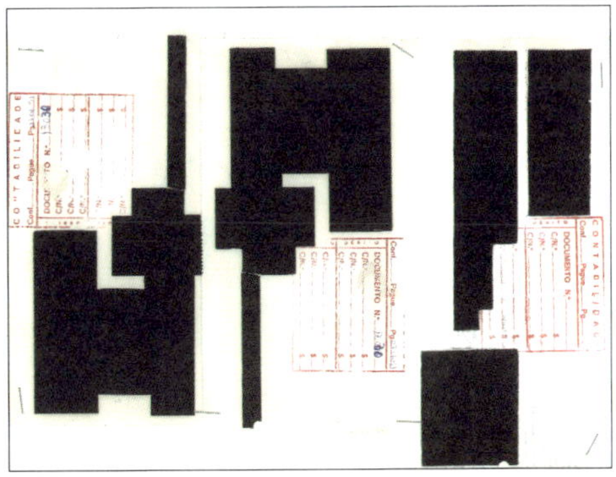

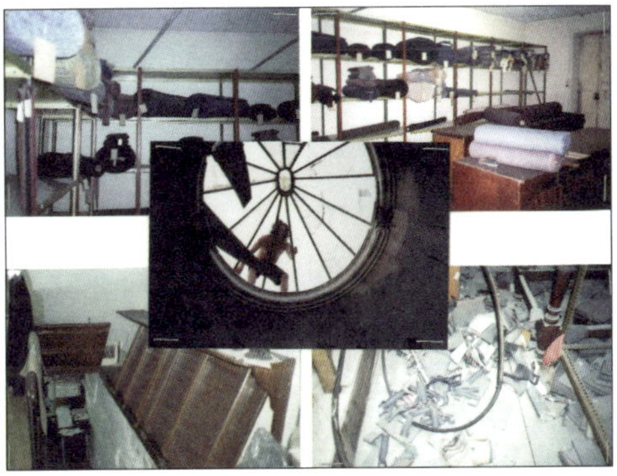

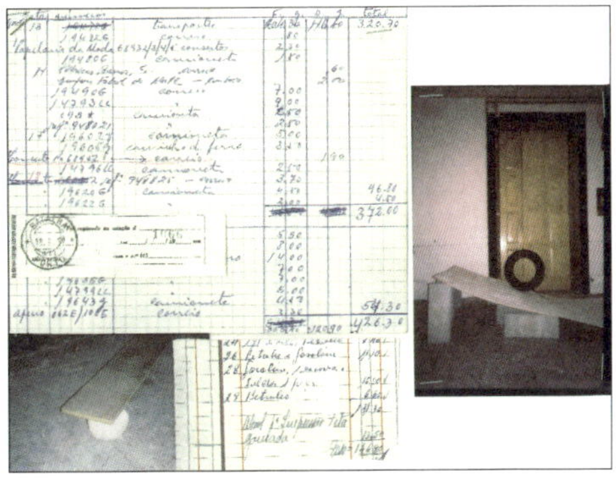

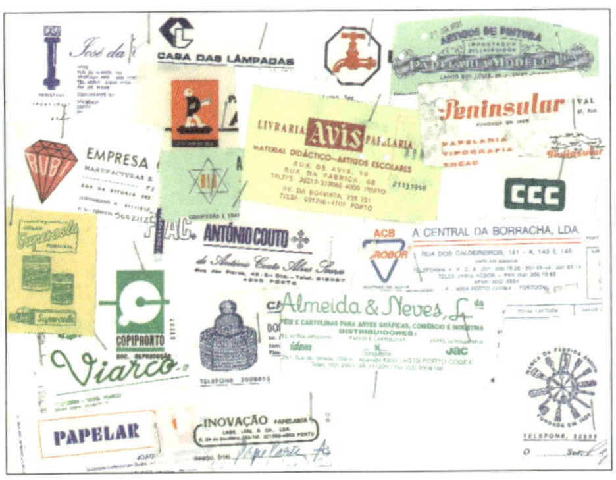

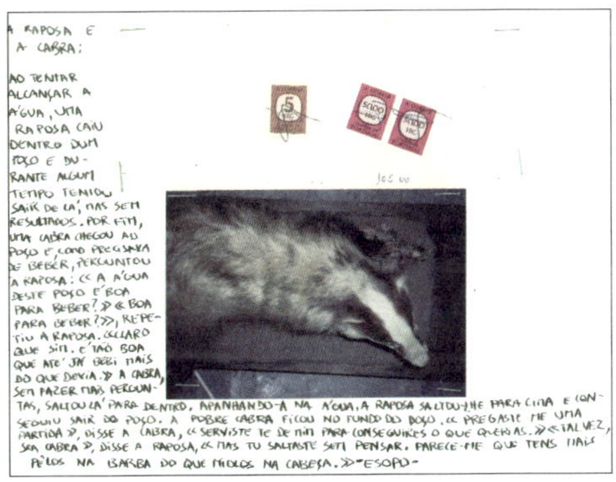

Postais do Porto
India ink and collage on paper
Series of 30 (23 x 31 cm)
2011

Postais do Porto is a series of pieces in which I make photographs of Oporto hold a dialogue with texts about the everyday life of the people living in the city centre. I've also added part of the accounts from a stationer's that was located in the same building as my workshop. Hence we find vestiges of an economically prosperous past together with the shortages of the present day.

Mauro Cerqueira

OS BANCOS ROUBARAM
DINHEIRO ÀS PESSOAS

DEVÍAMOS NÓS ROUBAR OS BANCOS.
OCUPAR AS CASAS QUE ESTES
ROUBARAM, ROUBAR OS COFRES.
E NINGUÉM FIC
PARA COMPRAR ARTE E PATROCINAR

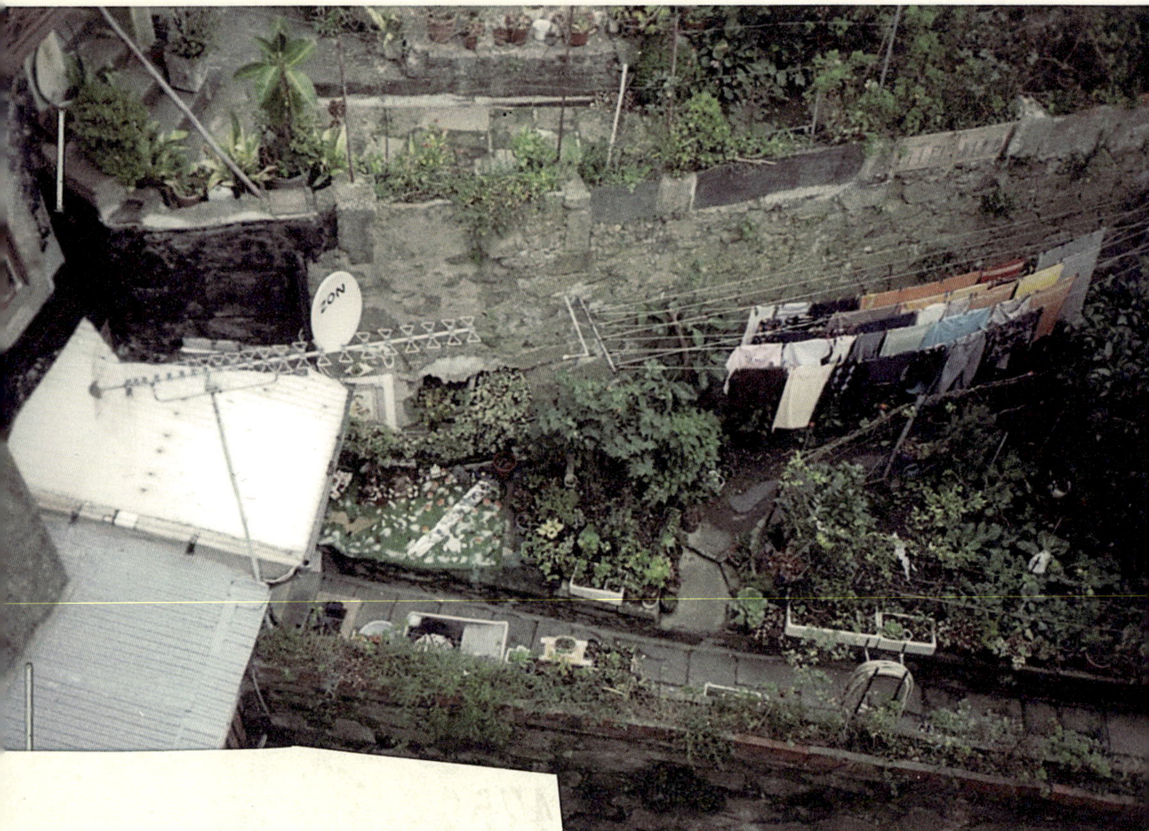

CREDITO PREDIAL PORTUGUES

BANCO BORGES & IRMÃO

DEPOSITAMOS

(VIDE DOSSIER)

BANCO PORTUGUES ATLAN

DEPOSITAMOS

(VIDE DOSSIER)

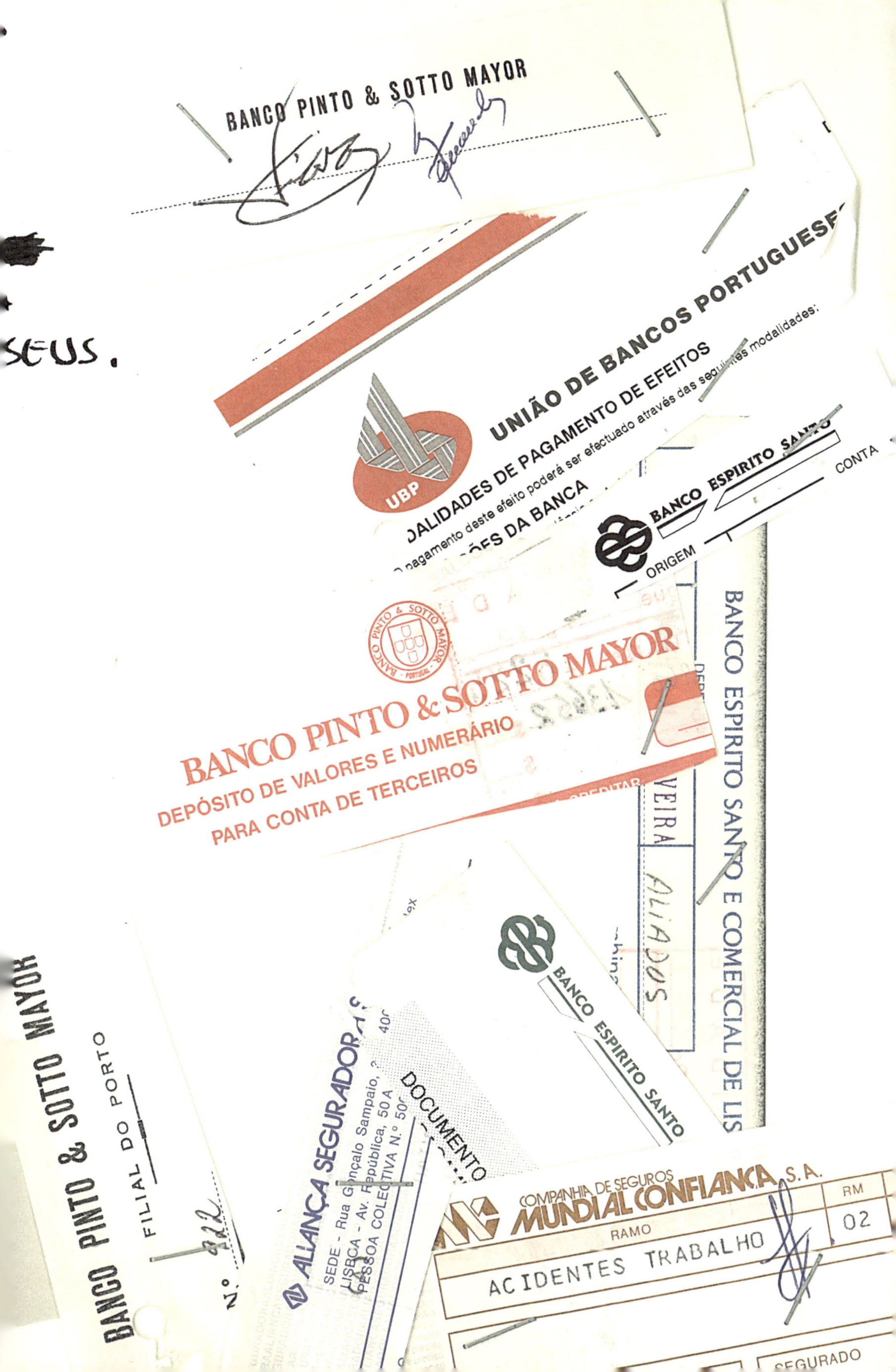
BANCO PINTO & SOTTO MAYOR
UNIÃO DE BANCOS PORTUGUESES
UBP
MODALIDADES DE PAGAMENTO DE EFEITOS
O pagamento deste efeito poderá ser efectuado através das seguintes modalidades:
BANCO ESPIRITO SANTO
CONTA
ORIGEM
BANCO PINTO & SOTTO MAYOR
DEPÓSITO DE VALORES E NUMERÁRIO
PARA CONTA DE TERCEIROS
BANCO ESPIRITO SANTO E COMERCIAL DE LIS
ALIADOS
BANCO ESPIRITO SANTO
BANCO PINTO & SOTTO MAYOR
FILIAL DO PORTO
N.º
ALIANÇA SEGURADORA
SEDE - Rua Gonçalo Sampaio,
LISBOA - Av. República, 50 A
PESSOA COLECTIVA N.º
DOCUMENTO
COMPANHIA DE SEGUROS
MUNDIAL CONFIANÇA S.A.
RAMO
RM
02
ACIDENTES TRABALHO
SEGURADO

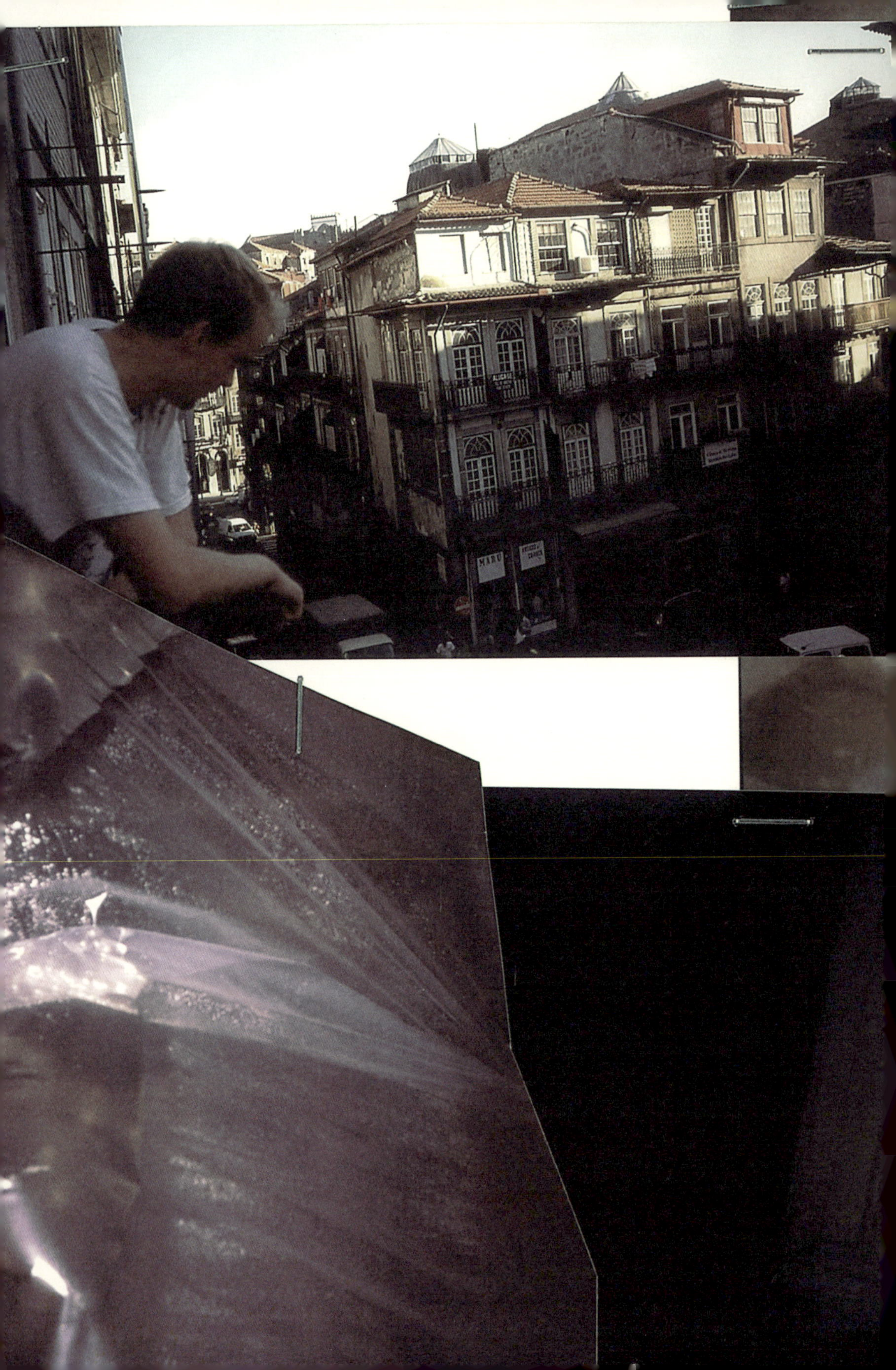
MARU

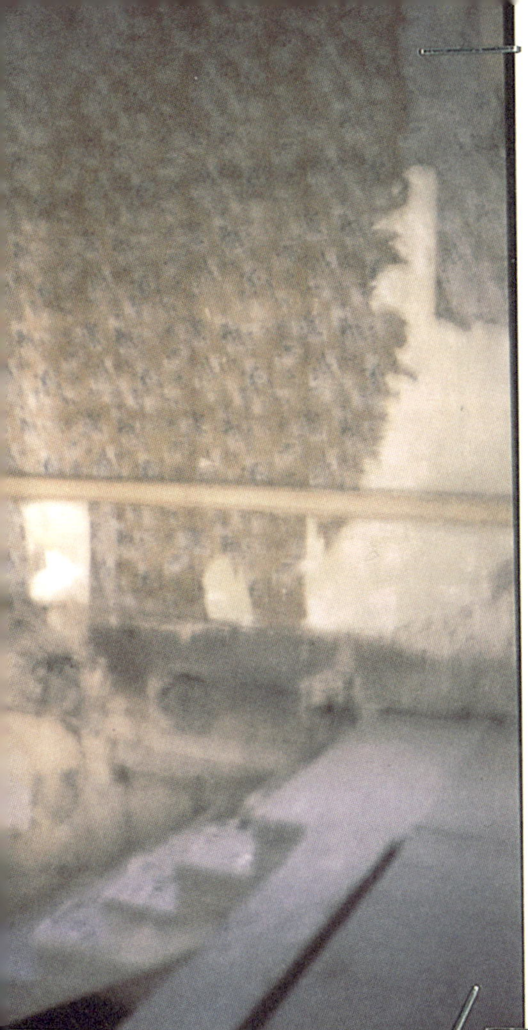

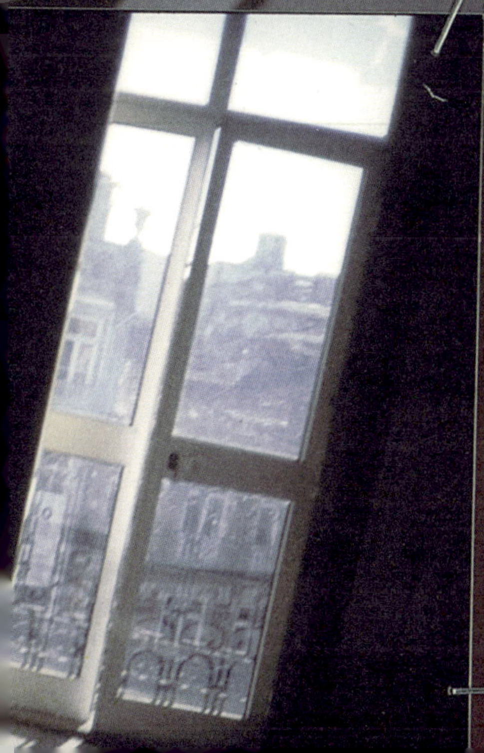

Shipwreck with spectator

Mauro Cerqueira (Guimarães, 1982) forms part of the youngest generation of Portuguese artists. Words such as tension, equilibrium, density, fragility and the pairing of destruction/construction define an artistic venture that's responding to the violence, stability and conformism of society. Cerqueira sees the public for his works as "the first witness to arrive at the scene of an accident". These are usually sculptural pieces and situations activated by the spectator, either because they result from a performance or because the installation is presented as the setting for a past or future action. A race on a bridge that is coming down or a construction made out of glasses about to topple are samples of work based on simple actions that give rise to precarious structures. The energy of youth and some references from subcultures such as punk and skate often leak into his work.

All these elements and attitudes are closely related to the historical, urban context in which Cerqueira has worked to date: namely the city of Oporto. Engulfed by the crisis suffered by the country for almost ten years now, this city in the north of Portugal has undergone considerable and rapid transformations. The decadence, ruin and misery of its old neighbourhoods, such as the Ribeira next to the River Duero, exist side by side with a project to modernise the urban fabric whose emblems are, for example, the new underground train network or the Casa da Música, designed by architect Rem Koolhaas. As these changes occur, the centre of Oporto is losing its inhabitants to make way for a growing tourism industry that is taking over these areas for commercial ends, in an all-too clear process of gentrification.

The two studios occupied by Mauro Cerqueira to date are located within this conflictive territory and have played a crucial role in the production of many of his works, redefining the patterns of site-specific practices. The first is located in a semi-abandoned building just a few metres from the city's most central square and close to one of the most degraded and problematic areas. From this studio, Cerqueira filmed the work *Até ao osso* in 2010. This video shows the excavation work carried out to construct the car park for a luxury hotel and the remains of an old cemetery that was dismantled. The anonymous star of the video, glimpsed by chance while the artist was looking out of his workshop window, is a young man, possibly someone living locally, who is prowling and rummaging around the graves, picking up bones and skulls which he puts into a plastic bag.

Até ao osso shows the destruction of a part of Oporto's old town, how it's under attacked from speculation, its inhabitants are being displaced and its history forgotten. Other works provide a different response to the same scenario. This is the case of many sculptures and installations closely related to the first studio, recently also a victim of real estate interests and decline. The *Trepadeiras* series (2010-2011), for example, is a collection made with pieces of shutters that are disassembled, lengthened and adjusted to different spaces and configurations. Using waste materials rescued from his immediate surroundings and with very simple gestures, Cerqueira creates new objects and situations that allude to instability and the impossibility of feeling safe within a context of perpetual transformation.

O cego e a cidade (2011), a recent video, acts almost as a farewell and homage to this place. It shows the end of a wooden stick hitting a plaster ceiling decorated with mouldings. The image is upside-down and the stick resembles a blind man's, examining the ground he's walking on. When the ceiling's material falls down, it instantly becomes a new element to work with. Destruction and construction therefore appear as metaphors for what's happening in the city: a rapid metamorphosis that's suffering from amnesia and a lack of interest in the past. Recording and conserving this harsh, unjust reality in the memory are always present in Mauro Cerqueira's work, together with a subtle, ironic sense of humour, as well as an enthralling, spontaneous expressiveness. Life and art are woven together in his work with authenticity and commitment, rejecting any temptation to turn misery into something picturesque. The precarious nature of an urban and social environment inspires his work to bring up existential uncertainties that go beyond any specific geography.

This vocation can be seen particularly clearly in a series of publications that constitute a fundamental part of his artistic work and bring together his interest in history, literature and popular culture. *Está a morrer e não quer ver* (2009), *Exvotos e milagres* (2009-2011) and *Momentos da história trágico-marítima e a Santa Liberdade* (2011) are publications produced in a newspaper-type format made up of drawings, his own and others' texts and documents from archives and libraries. In these Cerqueira explores Portugal's glorious past and its current fall from grace. In *Momentos da história trágico-marítima e a Santa Liberdade*, for example, fragments of texts from the chronicle by Bernardo Gomes de Brito in the 18th century, based on reports from survivors of shipwrecks occurring along the route to the Indies in the 16th century, are presented together with the history of the transatlantic ship *Santa Liberdade*; hijacked in 1961 by a group of Portuguese and Galician anti-fascists, led by the soldier Henrique Galvão, in an attempt to denounce the dictatorships of Salazar and Franco, which then went on to the African colonies with the aim, romantic and utopian, of starting a revolution that never actually prospered.

Illustrated with drawings by the artist to accompany the stories compiled by Gomes de Brito in 1735 and by a selection of the front pages of newspapers relating the ups and downs of the 1961 hijack, this publication recounts the origins of the Portuguese empire, an epic story full of adventurers, heroes and great seamen but also of shipwrecks, dramas and suffering, with the beginning of the end of their conquests, indicated, in this case, by the incident of the ship *Santa Liberdade* and its unsuccessful revolution. History, literature and fiction go hand in hand in an anti-hierarchical project, designed to be distributed beyond institutional channels and conceived as a mobilising and contemporary protest against forgetfulness.

On the back cover of *Momentos da história trágico-marítima* there is an extract from the book *Naufragio con espectador* (1995) by the German writer Hans Blumenberg, which summarises his intentions: "Montaigne does not justify the spectator of shipwreck by his right to enjoyment; rather, he justifies his pleasure, positively described as malicious (*volupté maligne*), by his successful self-preservation. By virtue of his capacity for this distance, he stands unimperiled on the solid ground of the shore. He survives through one of his useless qualities: the ability to be a spectator". Mauro Cerqueira's sculptures, videos and publications question, physically and conceptually, the existence of this distance.

Pedro de Llano
Exit Express, no. 60, 2011

Pepe Cifuentes

amb la col·laboració de

flo6x8

The possibility of the autonomy of art has constituted one of the great themes of debate of recent decades. The antagonism between those who sought the purity of artistic genres and those who, on the contrary, desired the complete absorption of art by life has been a constant and repeated phenomenon from the irruption of the avant-gardes to the present day. At the end of the 1950s, with the shift from a production-based society to one founded on consumption, it became evident that aesthetic experience and our own subjectivity formed a new territory for the expansion of capital. The separation between art and life dissolved, and art now had a purpose – not to achieve a better world, but simply to make economic profit.

In the face of this situation, a significant number of artists understood that artistic activity was inseparable from the administrative and political structure in which it was immersed, and furthermore, that there was no separation between the two. In the 1970s, artists like Hans Haacke or Michael Asher developed their work on the basis of these premises, in what finally became known as institutional criticism.

The hypertrophy of the institution of art from the 1980s and 1990s onwards finally absorbed a considerable number of these practices. And with the expansion of a now global market that affected the most diminutive aspects of our behaviour, the need for new strategies became evident. In recent years we have witnessed the emergence of groups of artists, including flo6x8, who, drawing on certain ideas of Michel de Certeau, seek an impact on our ordinary life, on what we tend to consider our "natural" life in spite of the fact that it has never been as constructed, as manipulated, as it is now. In this way, flo6x8 uses flamenco music and dance and other forms of popular expression to denounce the way our lives are being made more and more precarious, to a large extent by the excesses of our present-day financial system. Irony, humour and parody are other aspects that characterise the political agitation activity of this group that defines itself as "activist–artistic–situationist–performance-based–folkloric–non-violent." By means of their actions, in ATM spaces and bank branches, they produce discontinuities in our everyday life, overturning it and bringing the citizen in the street to centre stage. Their works lack the aesthetic autonomy that was demanded by the most orthodox modernity, over and above the interruption of our everyday existence. Proposals like those of flo6x8, so difficult to classify, are an essential stimulus for making art something closer and more necessary in an artistic system that sadly seems to be increasingly academicised and subjected to the laws of the market.

Yolanda Romero

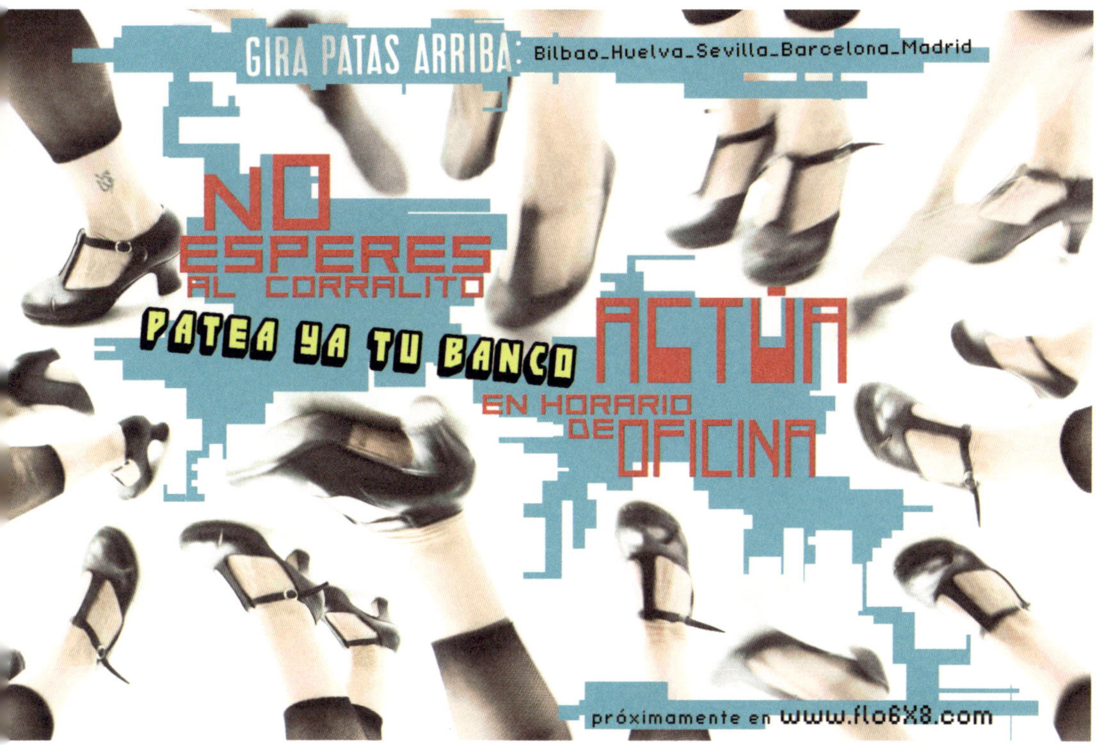

*"Banker, you've got money and I've got a flower vase,
You've got your wallet and I've got my umbrella stand..."*

*"'A Flamenco Musical against the Financial System.'
This is the subtitle of this documentary, and I ask myself:
Would I go into a cinema to see a film with a title like that?
I don't think so."*

Can_the_body_withstand_so_much_capital?

We all agree that "hitting a bank" is something very serious. It takes a lot of work, and to do it properly you have to be both bold and smart.

As a guide for developing the skill of "hitting a bank," in the tutorial that appears on the website of the group flo6x8, Chari Lee follows these steps: one, the plans; two, the trial runs; and three, the hit.

Neither all flamencos eat *puchero* in a wicker chair nor all bank robbers use a guitar case to hide their machine gun.

In the spring of 2010, a number of banks had already been used by the members of flo6x8 to carry out their actions. With no prior warning, out of the blue and always during office hours. This was the *Patas Arriba ["Upside-Down"] Tour*. Apart from those who were present in the branches at the time, very few people had got wind of their campaigns.

In that same spring, an anonymous source showed to a colleague at Camping Producciones the recording of one of the actions of flo6x8 captured by a bank's video surveillance camera. This recording was followed by more: "found material" that became "filtered material." With these recordings, we set to work gathering information on the actions and the people who performed them. This was how we came across www.flo6x8.com, the website that contains a large number of the group's videos, graphic material, invitations, texts, etc.

Having located them, we wrote to them proposing to make a documentary. To our surprise, they replied that their assembly had decided not to collaborate with us because they were "tired of being led on by the media." We insisted that our intentions were good, and that we had the video surveillance pictures of their actions. But we got no answer from them. We were missing the opportunity to do something of quality and with true meaning. Total crisis. Then someone suggested making a documentary with found material. We had the video surveillance pictures and the group's videos and website were open to the public. And that was how we produced the documentary on the basis of two sources: flo6x8.com itself and the panoptic, the subjective and the objective. We were convinced that once they saw the result, the approach of taking their pictures from the website would be well received.

One of the main ideas that we had in mind from the outset and that determined the course taken by the script over the months, through its various twists and turns, was to abstain from the use of witnesses that is so common in documentaries. The idea of defending a work that stands up on its own, without witnesses, became a kind of seal of identity, an element of style that we were committed to. Perhaps it was no more than a formal and rather risky wager of a team that knows it has such good material that it can afford to do away with narrative supports of a didactic nature. Although certain outside opinions made us waver more than once – apart from our own

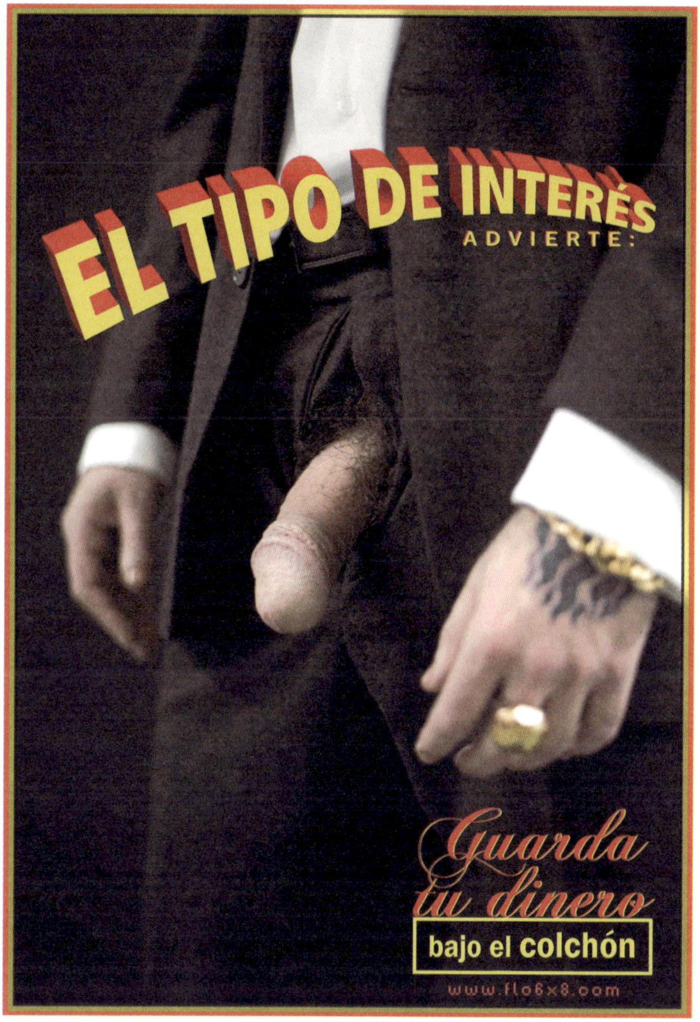

waverings – the pictures were so powerful that we were able to let them speak for themselves.

The circumstances restricted us at the start, forcing us to go back to the origins, to sit down and review the pictures and, although it may seem obvious, to question the classic format that we have used and reused so mechanically in the documentary genre.

Striving to be faithful to the philosophy of flo6x8, our goal in the documentary was to do away with labyrinthine discourses and stake everything on the nakedness of the music and the actions, keeping their meaning open. Appealing to the participation of the viewer, avoiding a closed, pedagogical discourse. In a nutshell, just like flo6x8, we preferred to reach debate through action, not the other way around.

Pepe Cifuentes, Camping Producciones
Seville, December 2011

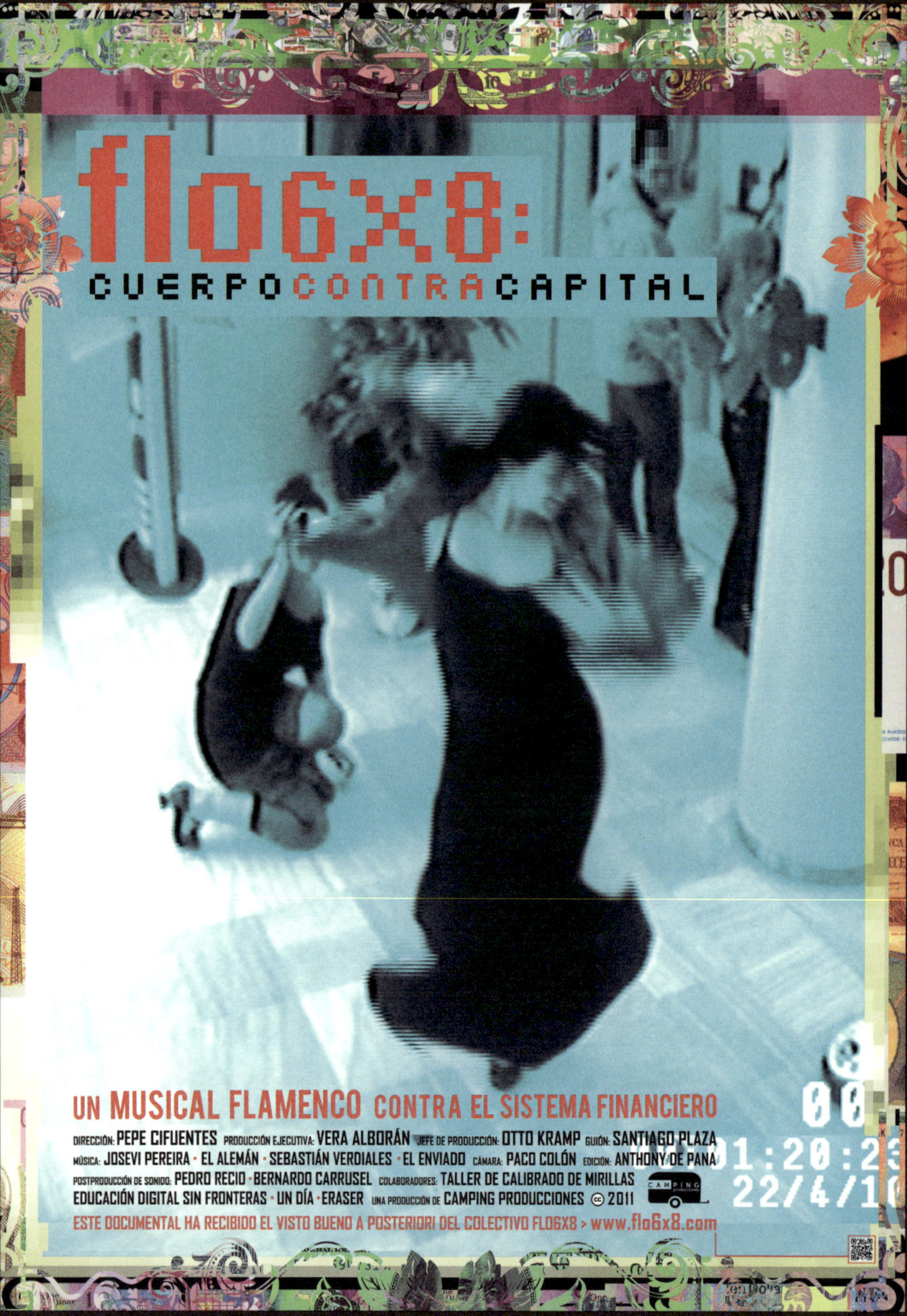
flo6x8:
CUERPO CONTRA CAPITAL
UN MUSICAL FLAMENCO CONTRA EL SISTEMA FINANCIERO
DIRECCIÓN: PEPE CIFUENTES PRODUCCIÓN EJECUTIVA: VERA ALBORÁN JEFE DE PRODUCCIÓN: OTTO KRAMP GUIÓN: SANTIAGO PLAZA
MÚSICA: JOSEVI PEREIRA · EL ALEMÁN · SEBASTIÁN VERDIALES · EL ENVIADO CÁMARA: PACO COLÓN EDICIÓN: ANTHONY DE PANA
POSTPRODUCCIÓN DE SONIDO: PEDRO RECIO · BERNARDO CARRUSEL COLABORADORES: TALLER DE CALIBRADO DE MIRILLAS
EDUCACIÓN DIGITAL SIN FRONTERAS · UN DÍA · ERASER UNA PRODUCCIÓN DE CAMPING PRODUCCIONES © 2011
ESTE DOCUMENTAL HA RECIBIDO EL VISTO BUENO A POSTERIORI DEL COLECTIVO FLO6X8 > www.flo6x8.com
22/4/10

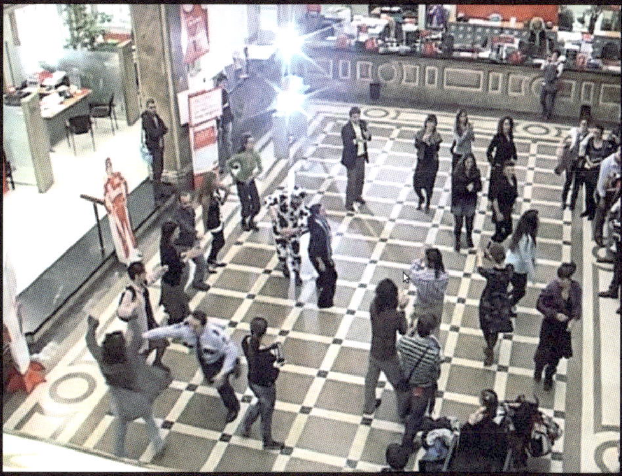

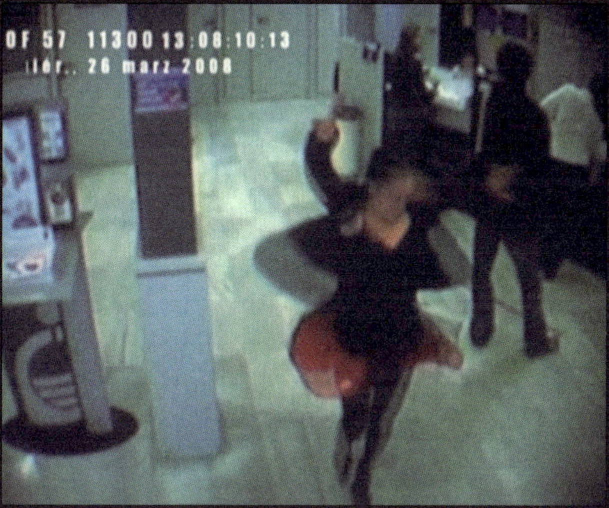

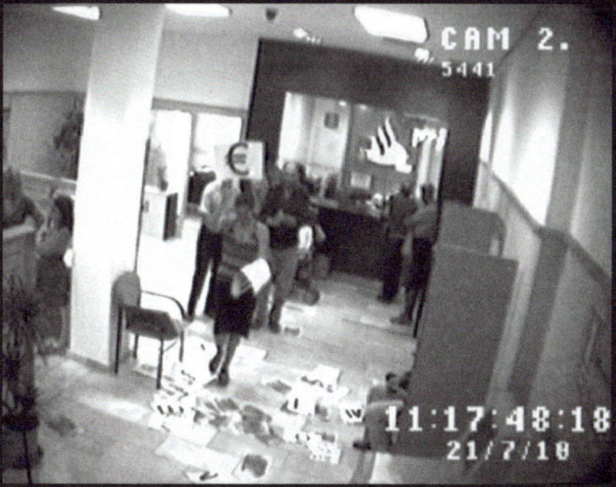

flo6x8:
Cuerpo Contra Capital. Un musical flamenco contra el sistema financiero
Video Documental
40'
Author: Pepe Cifuentes
Camping Producciones, 2011

The reception of the actions of flo6x8: the YouTube case

Among the critical observations we have received on our actions, we often hear this question: "Do you really believe what you do serves any purpose?" We will try to answer it on the basis of flo6x8's best-known action.

Censorship consists in an act of surveillance and control of expressions considered harmful. When censorship is exercised by the corporations called digital media conglomerates, such as YouTube (Google Inc.), at the urging of another corporation, for instance the Banco Santander, it has to be understood that the latter has suffered some type of harm to its public image.

The video "Rumba Rave 'Banquero' Flashmob" was posted on our YouTube channel on 16 December 2010. Just two days later, YouTube sent us the following mail, ordering us to remove or edit the video because it violated the privacy of certain "affected persons":

> *Dear flo6x8,*
> *This is to notify you that we have received a privacy complaint from an individual regarding your content:*
>
> *Video URLs: http://www.youtube.com/watch?v=gKJOmd9M8og*
> *The information reported as violating privacy is at 1:57, 2:01, 2:06, 2:11, 2:20, 2:25, 2:26, 2:40, 3:17.*
>
> *We would like to give you an opportunity to remove or edit your video so that it no longer potentially violates the privacy of the individuals involved You can edit your video by removing names and other personal information from the video's title, metadata or tags. Annotations or marking the video as private are not acceptable forms of editing and your video will still be at risk of removal. Please edit or remove the material reported by the individual within 48 hours from today's date. If no action is taken, the video will then come in for review by the YouTube staff and be prohibited from being uploaded again.*
> *If the potential privacy violation is contained within the metadata or title of the video, you should be able to edit this content without video removal. If the potential privacy violation is within the video content, the video may have to be removed completely.*
> *Protecting a person's privacy is protecting their personal safety. When uploading videos in the future, please remember not to post someone else's image or personal information without their consent. Personal information includes things like names, phone numbers, and email addresses. For more information, please review our Community Guidelines at http://www.youtube.com/t/community_guidelines and our Safety Center at http://www.youtube.com/t/safety*
>
> *Regards,*
> *The YouTube Team*

Studying the footage that allegedly infringed privacy, the "affected persons" turned out to be the security guard of the branch who appeared in the video.

It took only two days for the Banco Santander to become aware of the "threat" and complain to YouTube, and for the latter to send us the warning of closure of the video. Record time and immaculate diligence. As a result of the complaint, on 20 December 2010 YouTube removed the video. In just four days it had received 46,070 visits. On clicking on the link to the video, the following message appeared:

> *This video has been removed because its content violated YouTube's Terms of Service. Sorry about that.*

From that moment on there occurred what we would later come to know as "the Streisand effect": when a piece of information is censored in Internet, it rapidly becomes more widely disseminated. We could say that the Net was rebelling against this censorship, but a number of individuals had already downloaded the video in that short time, and on becoming aware of the censorship they uploaded it again to other YouTube channels and video platforms. While here at flo6x8 we were still wondering whether to upload it again ourselves with the staff's faces pixelled out (which finally we did), the news of the censorship was already spreading like wildfire in Internet and the new links to the copies of the video were beginning to circulate on blogs and a little later on the communications media. The copy that finally prevailed, in the YouTube channel of Wifigratis in January 2012, already has over 750,000 visits. Over 500 comments can be read under the video "Rumba Rave "banquero" en el Santander realizado por www.flo6x8.com" at http://www.youtube.com/watch?v=Wv5dh8v7mDs.

In the absence of a thorough semiotic analysis, the opinions expressed in these comments sent from far and wide reveal feelings of defencelessness, enthusiasm, indignation, disillusionment, hope, happiness ... But the most interesting thing they show is that this action by flo6x8 has inspired a number of people to take up stances on the political, aesthetic and ethical issues it raised.

If we wanted to analyse in depth the reception of the actions and campaigns of flo6x8, we would have to explore a number of different spheres: the communications media and social movements, the banks and institutions themselves, the world of art and culture, and more specifically flamenco, and so on. As with any cultural work, specific information of interest could be gathered on the repercussion of our proposal in all the fields it has reached. And also, naturally, on the social, political and economic situation and the social perceptions on the issues that pervade this action. As we do not have the necessary space here, we will let the collection of comments at the foot of the video suffice as an initial response to the question we quoted at the head of this text.

Paca la Monea, flamenco dancer and member of flo6x8

P.S.: Our Facebook profile has also been censored. "flo6x8 (figura pública)" is a misappropriation. Our profiles are "flo6x8 (organización sin ánimo de lucro)" and "Paca la Monea." Our YouTube video channel is www.youtube.com/user/flo6x8.

Patricia Dauder

Patricia Dauder's work is characterised by making conceptual explorations in the very genesis of images as a way of constructing new visions of reality that invert the processes of capturing it, in an attempt to return to a zero degree the adulterated forms of reality and replace them with an autonomous visual space where the act of seeing is de-subjetivised.

The film *Sporadic* shows black-and-white pictures of architectural sites under construction. A cadential sequence of zoom-ins and zoom-outs of the structure of the building generates an unreal movement that creates the false impression of a series of fixed images. The artist allows it to be the viewer's mind that has to reconfigure what it sees within this ceaseless oscillation of views that play with perception. Dauder's work forces the devices of recognition of reality in order to remind us that the "real" is no more than a construction of the mind.

The film *Flow* shows reflections of light off a standing surface of water. A succession of images of light and colour, recorded at dusk, flow and dissolve together, compressed in time. This space-time compression results in a continuous flow of light that deceives the viewer's eye with a seductive thematisation of luminic energy, above and beyond any external narrative to the cinematographic medium itself.

Patricia Dauder's *painting-drawings* stem from the same notion of "de-realisation" of the image. The artist works

and reworks them to the point of bringing about the dissolution of the image, in order for other meanings to appear which the viewer can add within the inconclusive patterns and the reiterated traces that do not seek to reconstruct any visible reality but merely to transport to the paper and the canvas something of her own experience in space and time. This gives them an intangible presence, fluctuating and at the same time active and necessary, in spite of the fruitless recognition of the images to which she may be referring, since they are above all explorations of the very act of making them emerge. The pictorial surfaces reveal themselves to the viewer's eye as pure emergences of the first vision of the things that transcribe their evolution above and beyond any appearance that may fix them.

Teresa Blanch

New York, May 2011

The body of my work, composed of drawings, films, canvases, three-dimensional objects and photographs, responds to an essentially visual investigation into the possibility of seeing and representing beyond the immediate setting, beyond the physical and objectual world. My creations are characterised by a marked procedural quality. Instead of being closed projects, they form part of cycles of research that extend in time, with the result that it is often difficult to establish limits, such as a beginning or an end, or to determine the separation between works. This procedural quality is accentuated by the idea of "fragment" that is evidenced both in the motifs – broken and incomplete shapes – that appear recurrently, and in the sketch-like appearance of the works.

This attempt to materialise the immaterial, to give shape to the shapeless, has given rise to a series of concepts related with time and space: the concept of pure vision, a space without parameters and the idea of *continuum* as an endless process. For me, both time and space are highly fragmented dimensions that cannot be delimited or contained. I conceive of time not as the consequent linear passage of a series of events, but as a dimension, or multiple dimensions, in which diverse realities occur simultaneously. Likewise, my concept of space is not subject to measurements: it is infinite, multiple, layered, and it expands from micro- to macro-structures, from diminutive objects to enormous extensions that surpass our optical and perceptive capacities. This is linked in turn to the idea of a pure vision, as a kind of metaphysical vision, with light as an important symbol for seeing beyond the immediate.

There are three starting points or positionings that I make use of in my current work:

> The observation of the physical world and an interest in the phenomenological and metaphysical dimension of reality, which I develop through recording and recreating perceptible and non-perceptible matter, structure and change, space and time.

> The introspection and exploration of a psychological dimension, less conscious or rational, which manifests itself in morphologies, structures and visions that do not have a clear logic or continuity. To a large extent, I have developed this aspect through drawing, although more recently I have used sculpture and film. I understand film as a reflection of the reaction of my senses and a less rational form of thought regarding my surroundings.

> The autonomy or self-referentiality of the artistic object that I produce. The changes that take place in the images and objects that I create appear to evolve independently of my idea and my will, and the work becomes an autonomous entity.

When drawing the first lines in the white space of the paper, capturing something with the camera or modelling a form in space, I start out from an incipient mental projection of subjective perceptions or sensations that I am unable to represent with a clear morphology. This is the start of a long manufacturing process that runs in parallel with an equally long process of recognition of the image or object. Through the interrelationship between strokes and patches, light and colour, empty and full spaces, the form gradually imposes itself and dictates the steps to be followed. A dialogue is established between the presently existing form and what it evokes, a successive approaching-and-distancing movement between the idea and the material.

The viewer's meeting with my work follows a similar process. There is no narrative source, no story or concrete theme to go by. The public exhibition of the work is presented as a collection of images of diverse natures: drawings, moving pictures, projection of films or slides, and sculptures, which create a composition without hierarchies or delimited links. In spite of the fragmented presentation, a microcosm of multiple associations and iconographies is generated, probably a reflection of my own associative instinct, not analytical but rather poetic. Only through unhurried observation can the viewer perceive subtle meanings and possible connections: the relationship between opposites, negative and positive, mass and void, construction and destruction, the visualisation of the internal structure of bodies, organic or architectural, the reiteration of the radial circular form, representative systems such as maps and cosmologies, environmental phenomena that occur on a small or large scale, in brief instants or over very long periods of time, biomorphic shapes and natural elements that intermingle with references to the cinematographic support.

Patricia Dauder

Event
Graphite on paper
Drawing in two parts (67 x 95 cm each one)
2009

A picture consisting of two separate units which at the same time present a second partition drawn on the sheet of paper which breaks up a unitary vision. Nothing is represented here, but the title refers to an incident or happening that we do not see. An irregular gradation of blacks and greys and the fragmentation of the space of the paper itself give rise to a certain cinematographic impression.

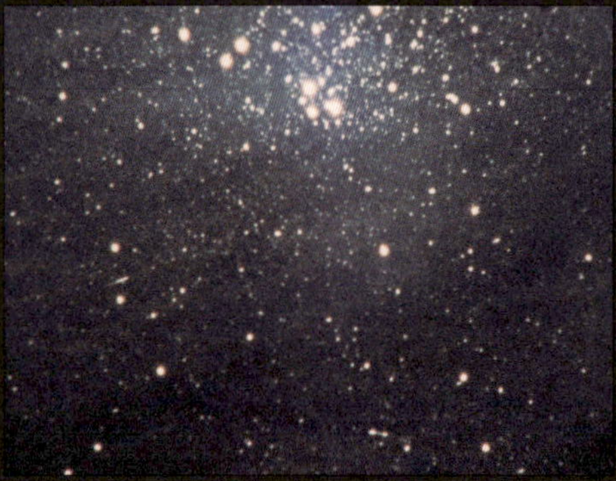

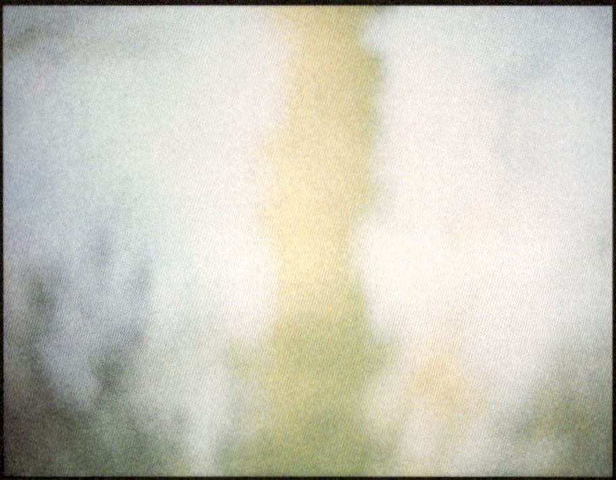

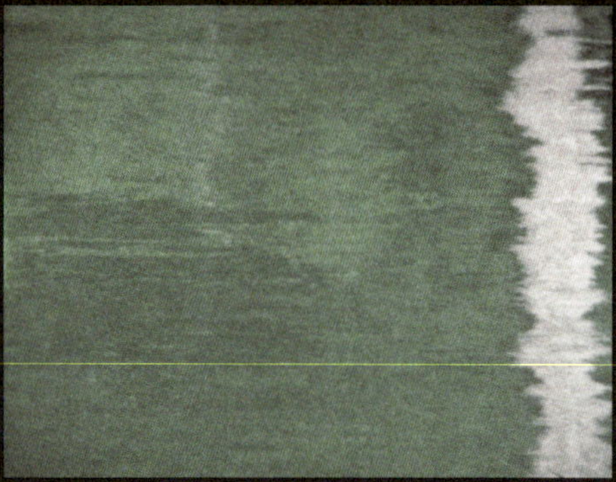

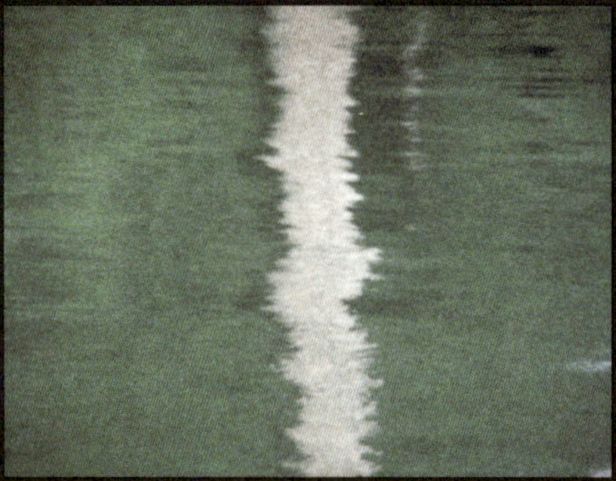

Flow

S8mm film transferred to 16mm
Colour, silent, 4'5"
Ed. 3 + 1 AP
2009

Flow explores the possibilities of observing basic materials like water and air. The film shows bright reflections of light on the surface of standing waters and a succession of transitions of light and colour at dusk, compressed in time. The different images succeed each other smoothly in a kind of constant flow of light that gradually darkens and lightens, creating a sensation of instability of vision, a hypnotic gliding effect. *Flow* focuses on the changes of light observed in nature and modified by optical and cinematographic mechanisms used to create spaces, which, as in the drawings, gradually expand and contract.

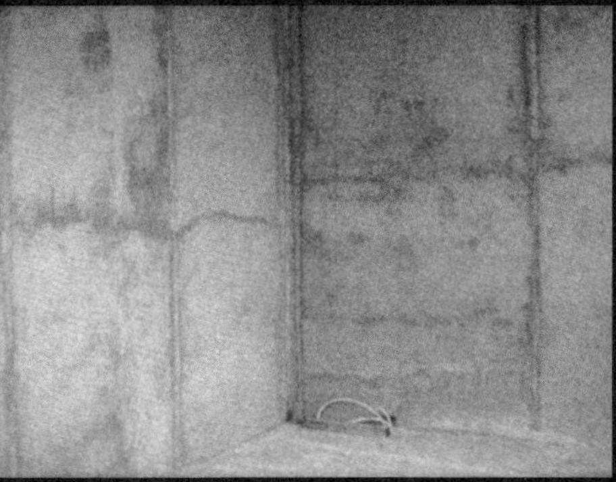

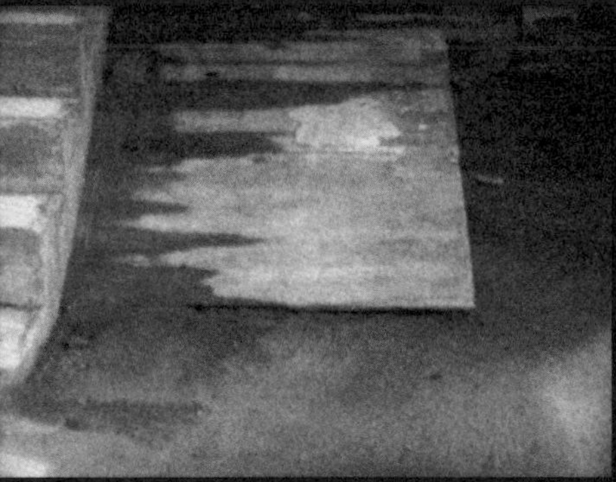

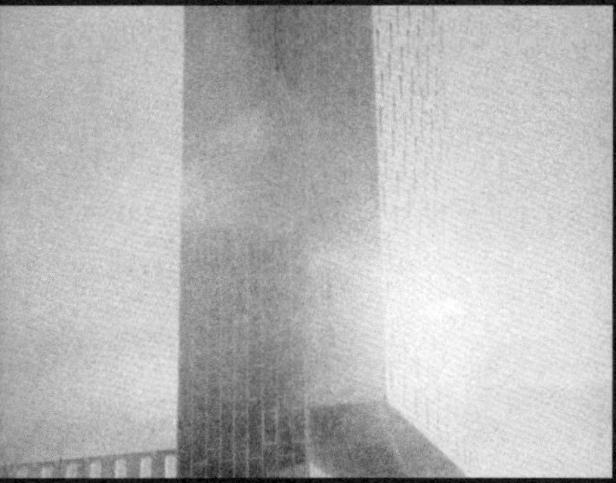

Sporadic

S8mm film transferred to 16mm
Black and white, silent, 4′ 25″
Ed. 3 + 1 AP
2009

Sporadic shows parts of buildings under construction whose interior structure is open and visible. The film is composed of 46 different shots that range from wide-angle to macro views. Neither the camera nor the subject move, so we have little evidence that we are looking at a film and not a photograph. The sequence of pictures is based on successive zoom-ins and zoom-outs, in such a way that our vision enters and exits the structure of the buildings at a fairly mechanical rhythm, with a change of picture every seven seconds and without transitions or fades. In spite of the apparent lack of motion, a certain degree of movement is created due to this regular, basic tempo of change of non-correlative fragments, and the viewer is led to imagine the spaces that do not yet exist, as in a jigsaw puzzle where pieces are missing. The film becomes a space in which we move both visually and mentally.

Plymouth
Graphite on paper
127 x 97 cm
2011

>
Untitled (Dusk N.Y.)
Bleach on canvas
172 x 128 cm
2011

The drawing *Plymouth* and the canvas *Untitled (Dusk N.Y.)* belong to a group of works commenced in February 2011 that revolve around the idea of the poster as a graphic and symbolic expression of the idea of paradise. These are images with little descriptive content but based on my personal perception of maritime settings where I have been or would like to visit, that have a historical relevance or a special significance in the culture of surfing and sailing.

The images are created in graphite on paper or using bleach on monochrome canvases, working with a colour subtraction method. The pictures are named after places. For instance, Plymouth (a town in the state of Massachusetts where the New England settlers established their first colony), Montgat, Rockaway or Montauk (localities close to Barcelona and New York where I regularly go surfing), or Hanalei, a beach on the north coast of the island of Kauai in the Hawaiian archipelago. Some of the places I refer to in an abstract manner in the drawings and paintings also appear in film projects.

Patricia Dauder

Carla Filipe

Carla Filipe has a wealth of expressiveness when penetrating the universe of drawing and work on paper that she tackles in her pieces, frequently in installations and artist books. She integrates both public and private aspects in her projects, creating a world that is referential but also mysterious, in which unexpected meanings emerge. Her techniques get away from the lineal format so characteristic of drawing, developing in any part of three dimensional space.

Vicente Todolí

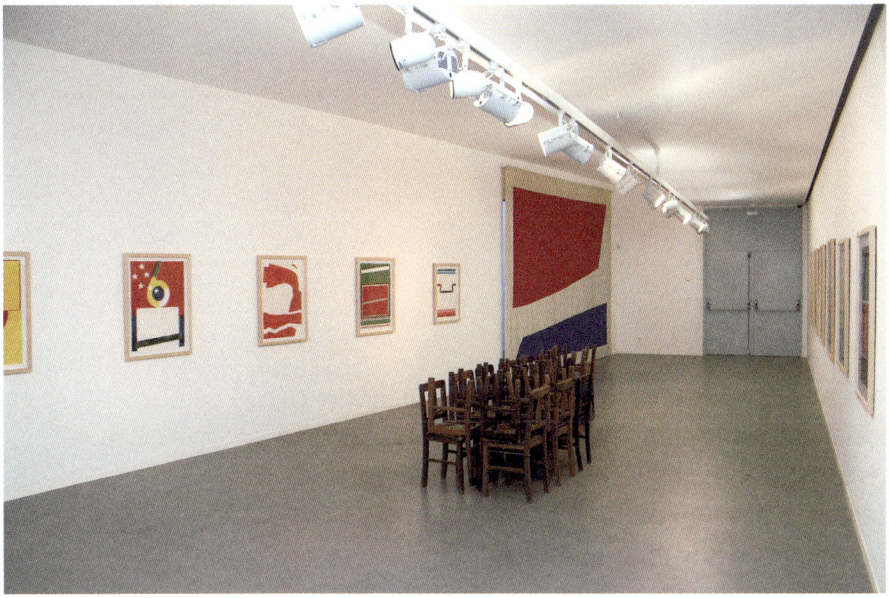

O Povo reunido jamais será - Representações gráficas
18 paintings (acrylics on paper; eight of 110 x 74 cm,
four of 84 x 63.5 cm, four of 98 x 72 cm, one of 85 x 56 cm
and one of 73.5 x 56 cm) and 18 chairs
2009-2011

In *O Povo reunido jamais será - Representações gráficas* (2009-2011) I continue a series of pieces whose basis is the archive of CGTP posters (General Confederation of Portuguese Workers), focusing on posters before and after the revolution of the 25th April 1974.

On reproducing them pictorially using acrylics on paper, removing the textual element of the poster, I call up a recent past in which the word brought individuals, groups or collectives together around political, social, economic and cultural causes.

In this work, *O Povo reunido jamais será - a espera,* I wonder about the current disassociation between words and image, the power of images, the outcome of removing words from an image, and observers can speculate on the image that the words, in isolation or together, might invoke today.

Carla Filipe

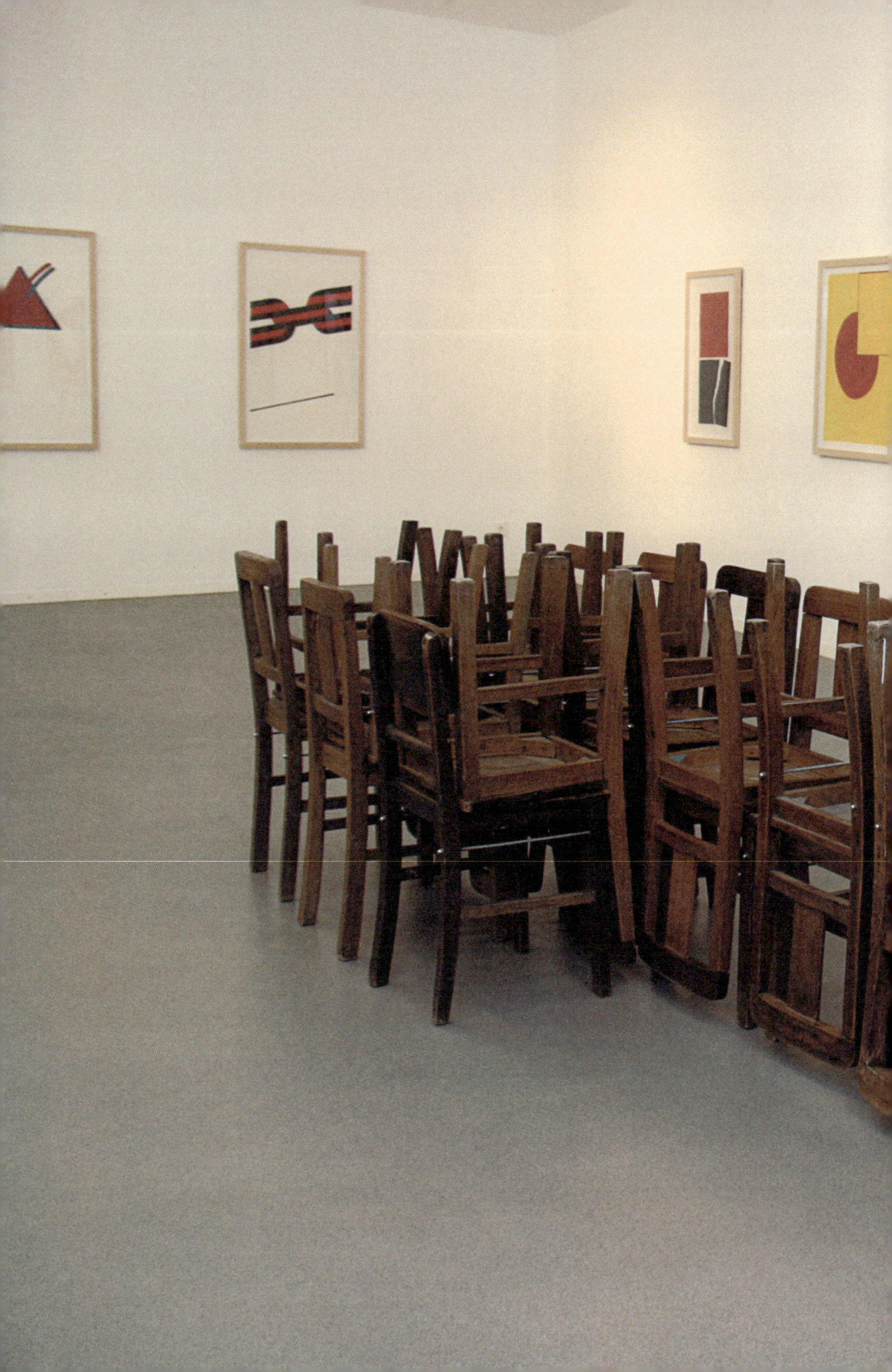

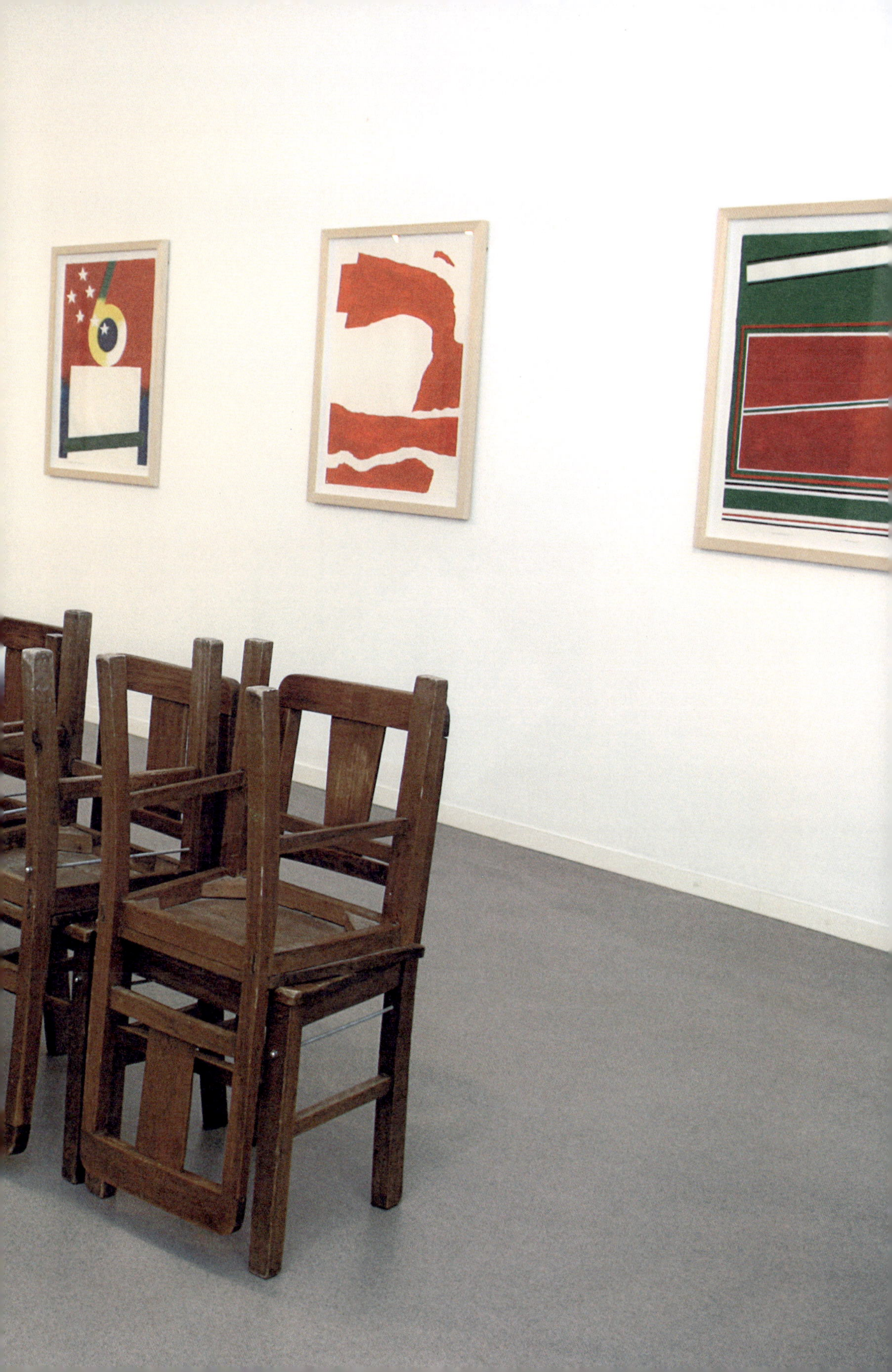

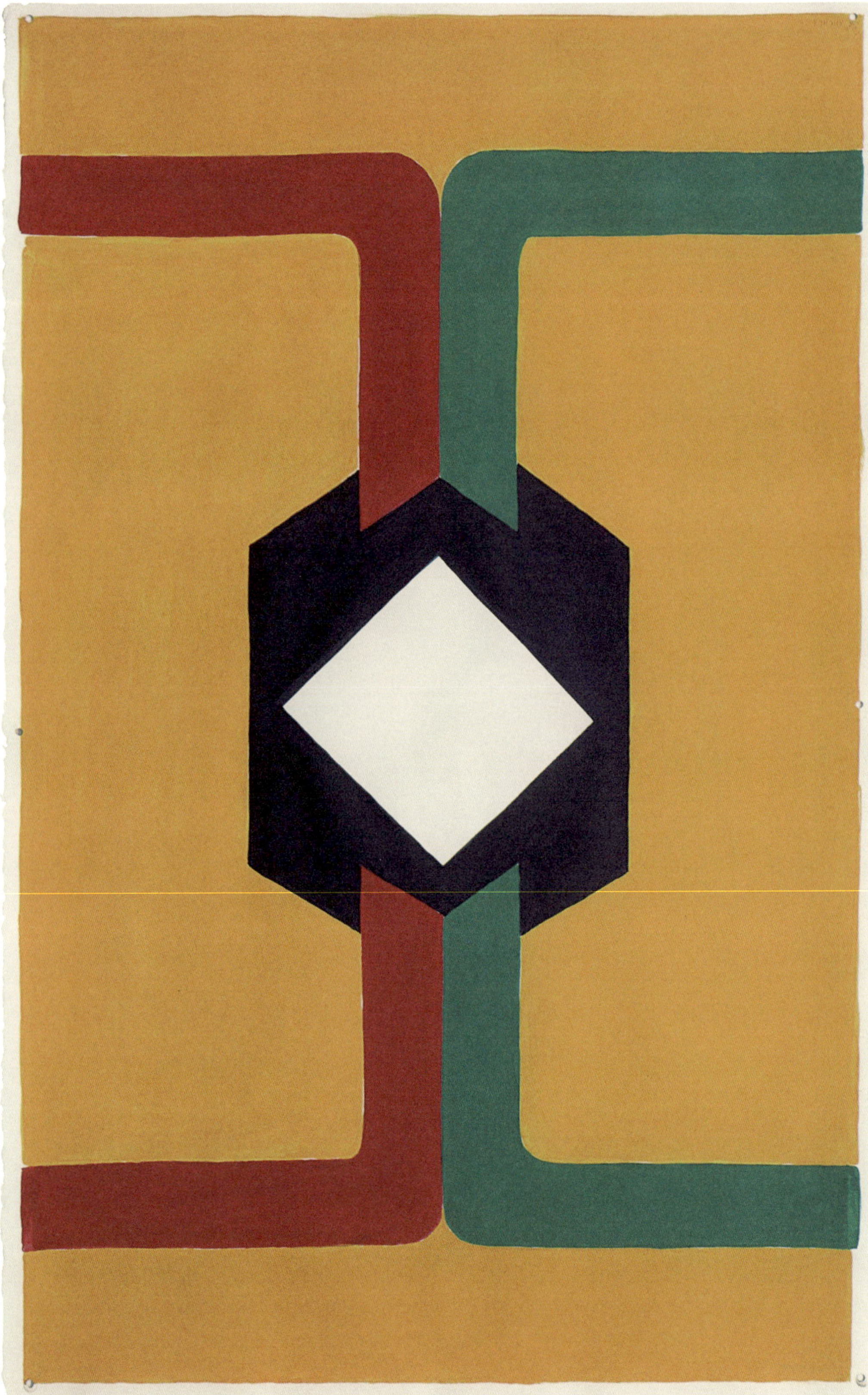

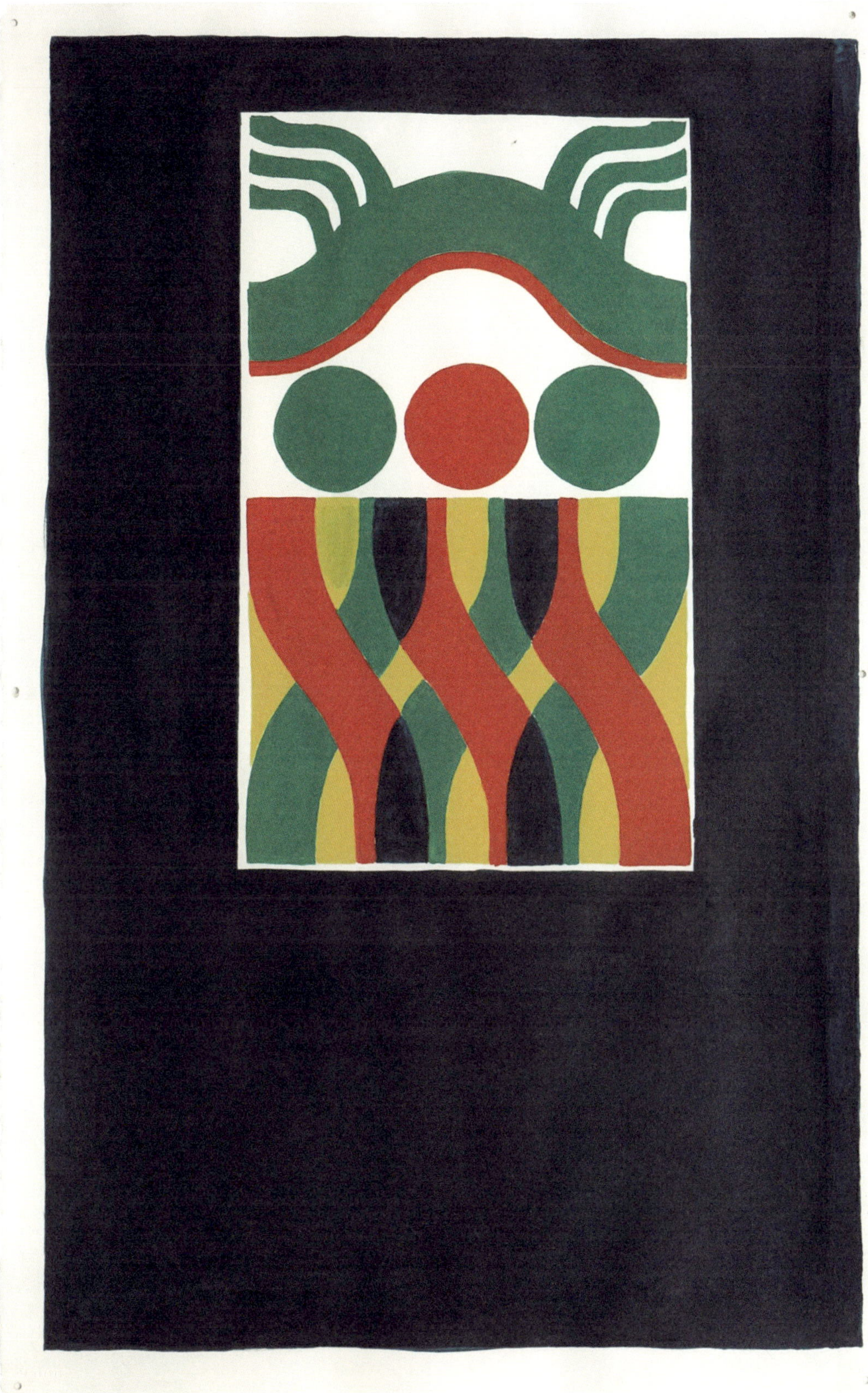

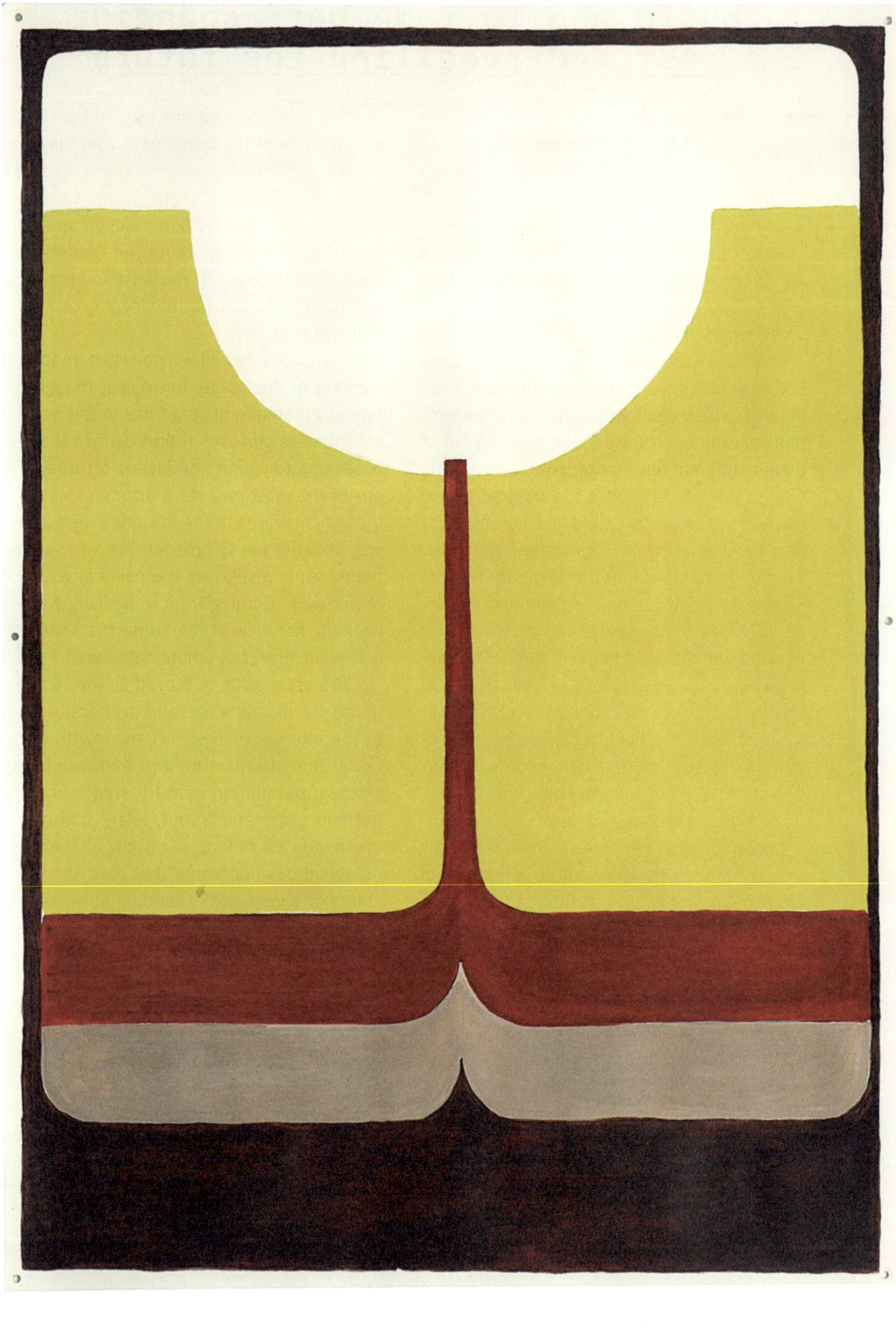

To build and to remember: changing the past and recalling the future

Carla Filipe's work focuses obsessively on memory (which may be personal and political, and/or syndical and artistic). This artist's references to a very specific universe (the railways) become universal when she quotes from political/syndical apparatus (flags, posters) or from historical sources (by displaying real and fictional documents).

Her work makes use of a set of codes and conventions from mass communication. It does not, however, resort to any techniques from Pop Art, which deals with advertising conventions to exalt or criticise them, creating out of them a different representational reality. Carla Filipe's work develops itself in the tradition of politically interventive art. Mass communication codes are equally important, but they explore other stimuli and are aimed at other objectives. The posters, flags, pamphlets, manifestoes or newspapers she uses do not illustrate the manifold forms of promoting consumer goods in an industrial or post-industrial society, but rather the different levels of political discourse (syndical, social, testimonial or purely political) that directly or indirectly, partially or totally put into question the foundations of that very same society.

Carla Filipe's body of work grows out of the history of the living and working conditions of the popular masses, just as they can be understood within the context of the industrialisation during the 19th century and most of the 20th. 1800s realism, some forms of expressionism from between the two world wars and the various forms of socialist realism, and also the deconstruction of these traditions, within the dominant context of structuralism, by Debordian situationism, present, over the vast historic and social time we have mentioned, a variety of ideological and formal approaches to the subjects and images testifying to the life and struggle of the oppressed classes.

This long tradition stands behind Carla Filipe's work; however, she avoids the simple quoting, reclassifying and spatial reordering of the signs of the political or everyday discourse that characterise much of what we could call 'sociological art': most of the elements in her work remain autonomous from any programmatic or reductive readings, or else disrupt, via her formal and technical approach to the image, the linearity of a mere political reading.

The biographic dimension is an important element in this ability to exceed; though not the only thematic driving force in the work, it nonetheless suffuses it and defines it as an obsession to which she always returns; it is one of the most important distinguishing and individualising features in Carla Filipe's oeuvre, allowing her to broaden her intervention fields, while displaying the political vocation of her work. Coming from a family of railway workers, her view of the subject is historical and subjective, but emotional as well.

The essential role played by the railways in the rise of capitalism and the development of the internal market, urban growth, traditional industrialisation and the proletarian classes, population mobility (redistributing national populations and, later, acting as a means to emigration), the study of the technological developments that gave them the status of a veritable expanding universe and the analysis of their decadence, the connections of this innovative form of transportation with the workers' struggles, combined with the study of the conservative, petty bourgeois and folksy mindset of its staff members, are some of the fields explored by Carla Filipe's work.

João Pinharanda
Prémio EDP Novos artistas 2011,
Assírio & Alvim, Lisbon, 2011,
pages 40-41

Nuria Fuster

Nuria Fuster focuses on the proximity of objects by making deconstructive compositions that are incredibly serious in formal terms. Structured and firm, her work has industrial connotations and is influenced by German sculptors. Recycling is essential to carrying out her work: paying attention to the objects around us and granting them their own status.

In the artist's own words: "My work can be summed up as a constant search for what's "real" in "reality". I'm interested in an object as something to be observed and as an exercise or act where the muscle to propel us towards it. It's about breaking the increasingly dark glass that separates us from it. An object as a structure acts as a mirror; if we can reach it, we get closer to our own nature".

The plasticity of the forms achieved and their visual beauty are two of the many qualities of her work, in which she deals with concepts such as distortion, vision, reduction and speed. Nuria Fuster has managed to create her own substantial grammar that goes deeper into the relations of the subject with its most immediate surroundings. Furniture and disused objects are her raw material and process is her resource. She achieves her aim while also leaving the door open to chance, handling what is accidental and what is necessary as if it were a demiurge.

María de Corral

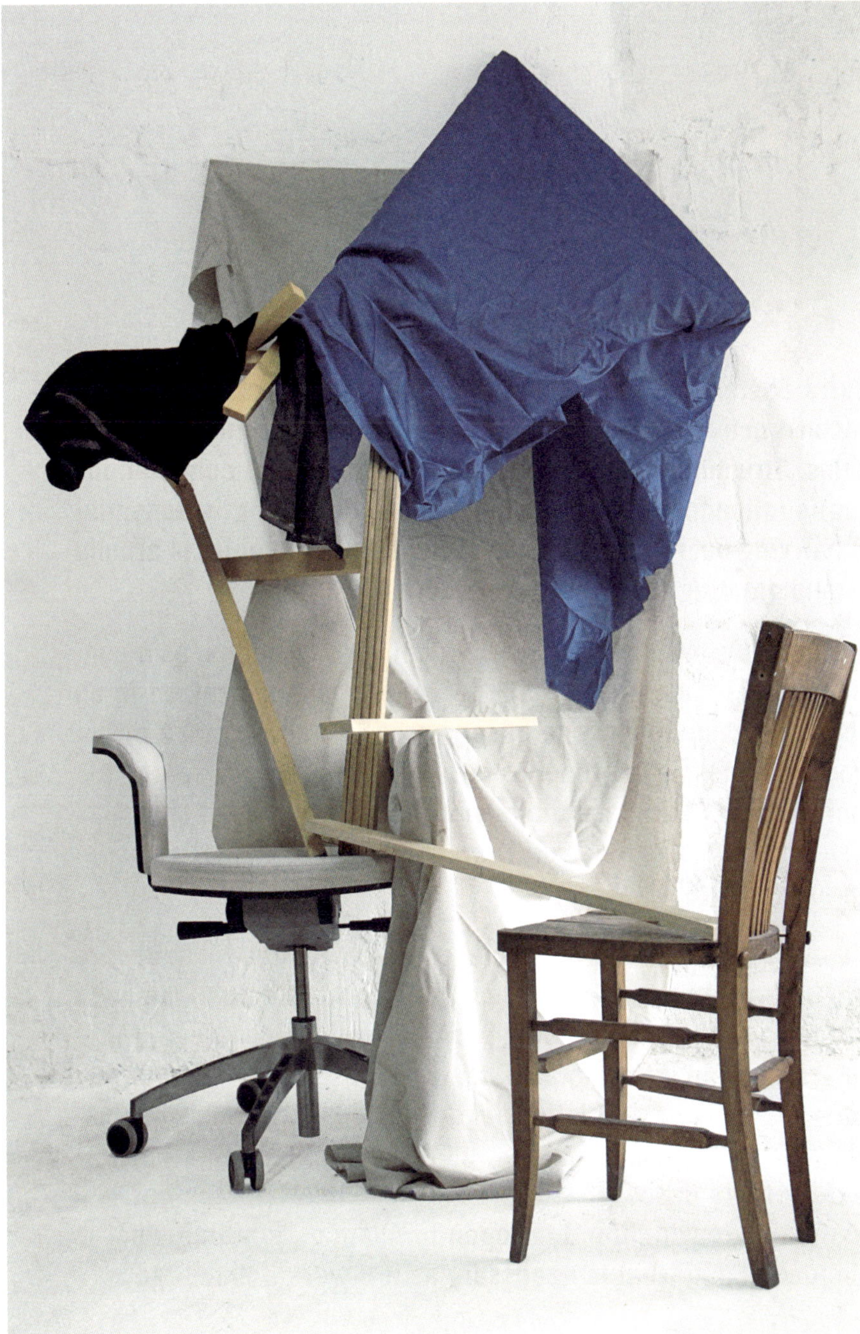

Estado 1
Lambda photographic print
110 x 76 cm
Series: 1/5
2011

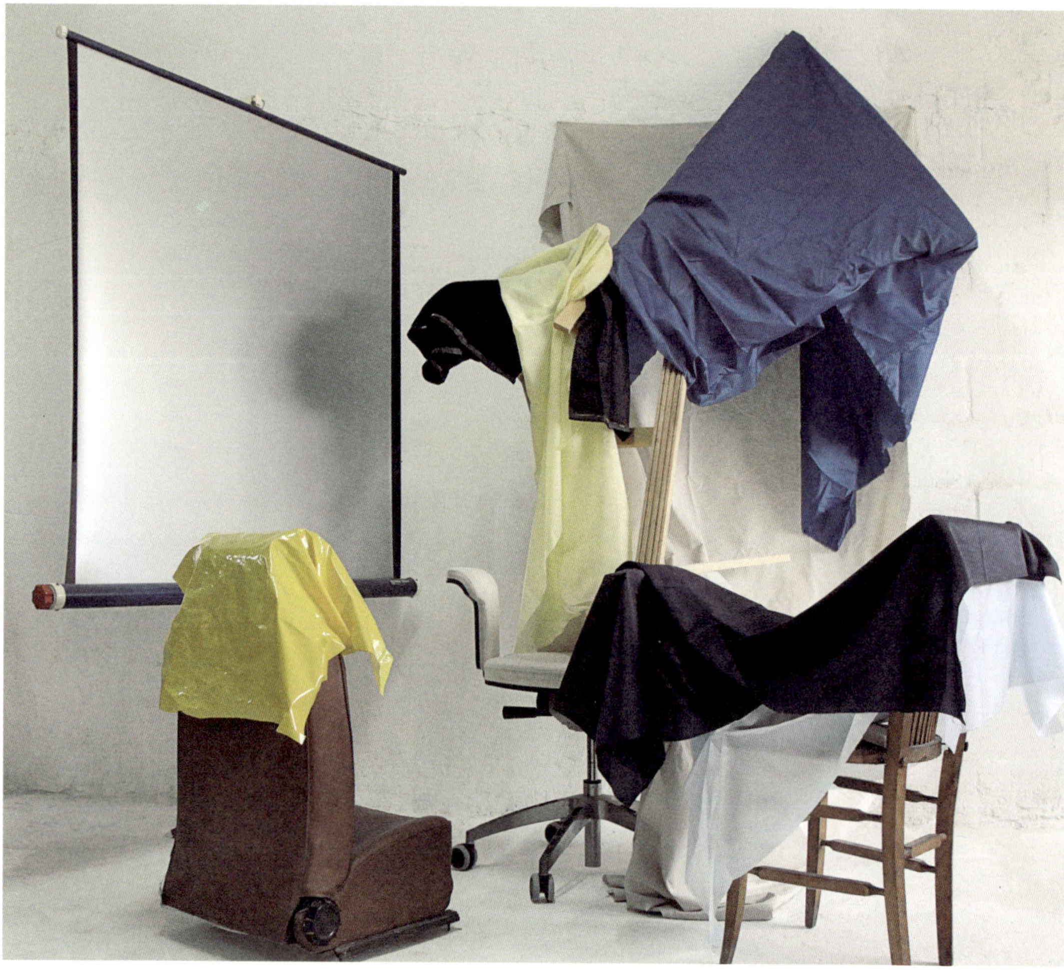

Estado_2
Lambda photographic print
110 x 97 cm
Series: 1/5
2011

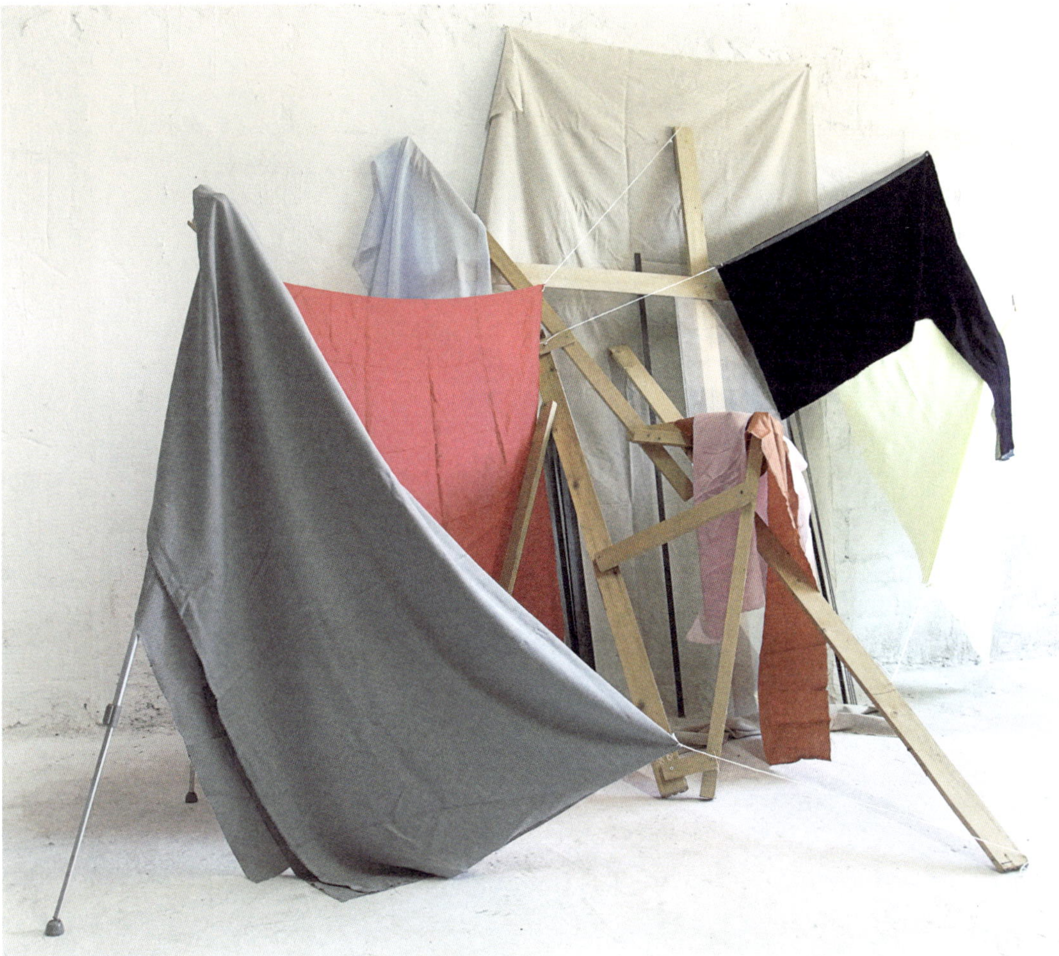

Estado_9
Lambda photographic print
110 x 93cm
Series: 1/5
2011

Rawness, heart, the core

My goal isn't to represent but rather present. My daily work in the studio is an exercise in clearing out everything that has been said and done, placed onto things. They are solitary encounters with each object, with each material as if it had never been made for anything. I believe they potentially conceal a nature I want to find out about and I'm interested in this origin.

These pieces come from differentiated projects but they all contain a dialogue between sculpture and painting. Colour as a constructive element, as another physical material.

Nuria Fuster

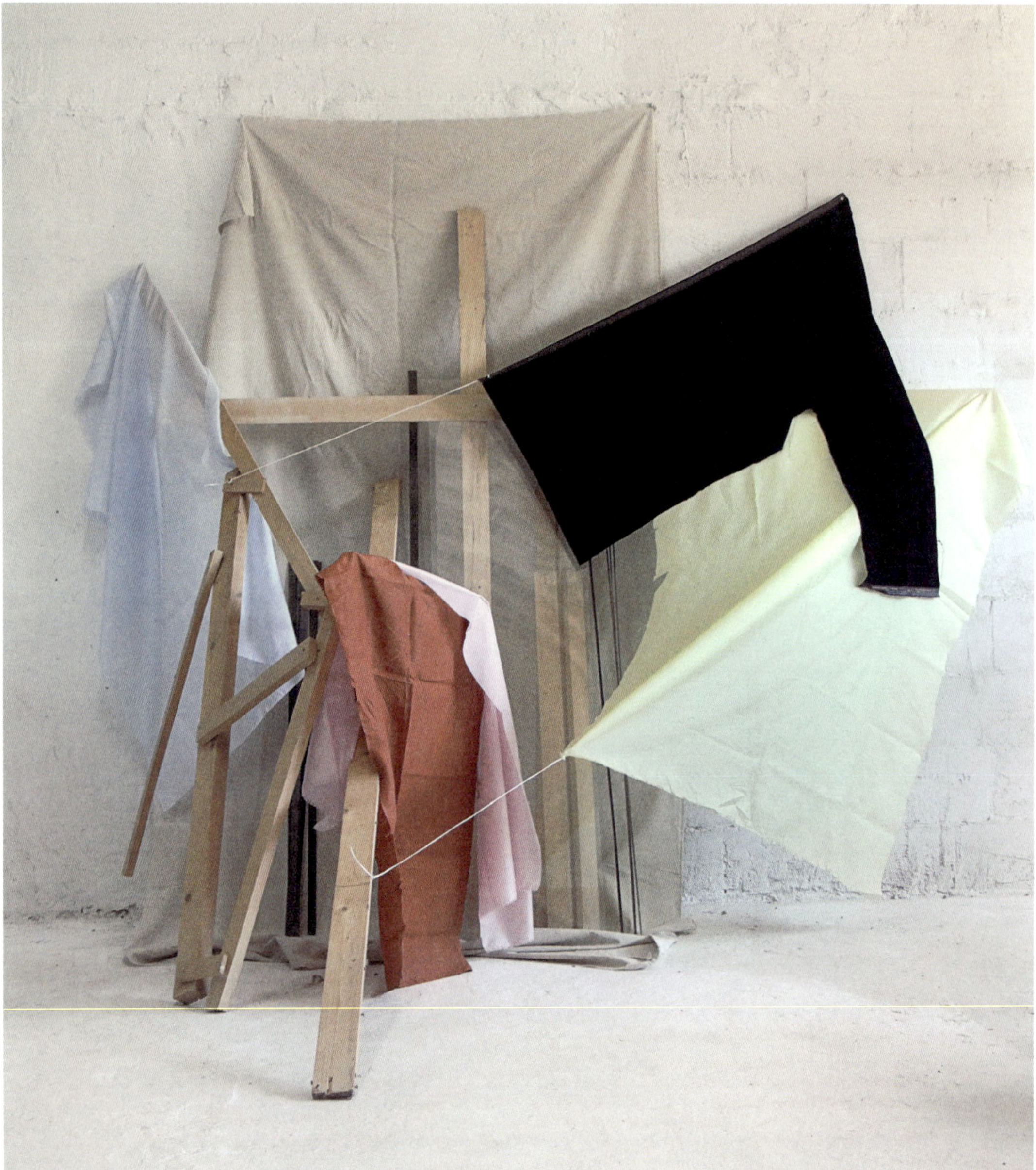

Estado_7
Lambda photographic print
110 x 100 cm
Series: 1/5
2011

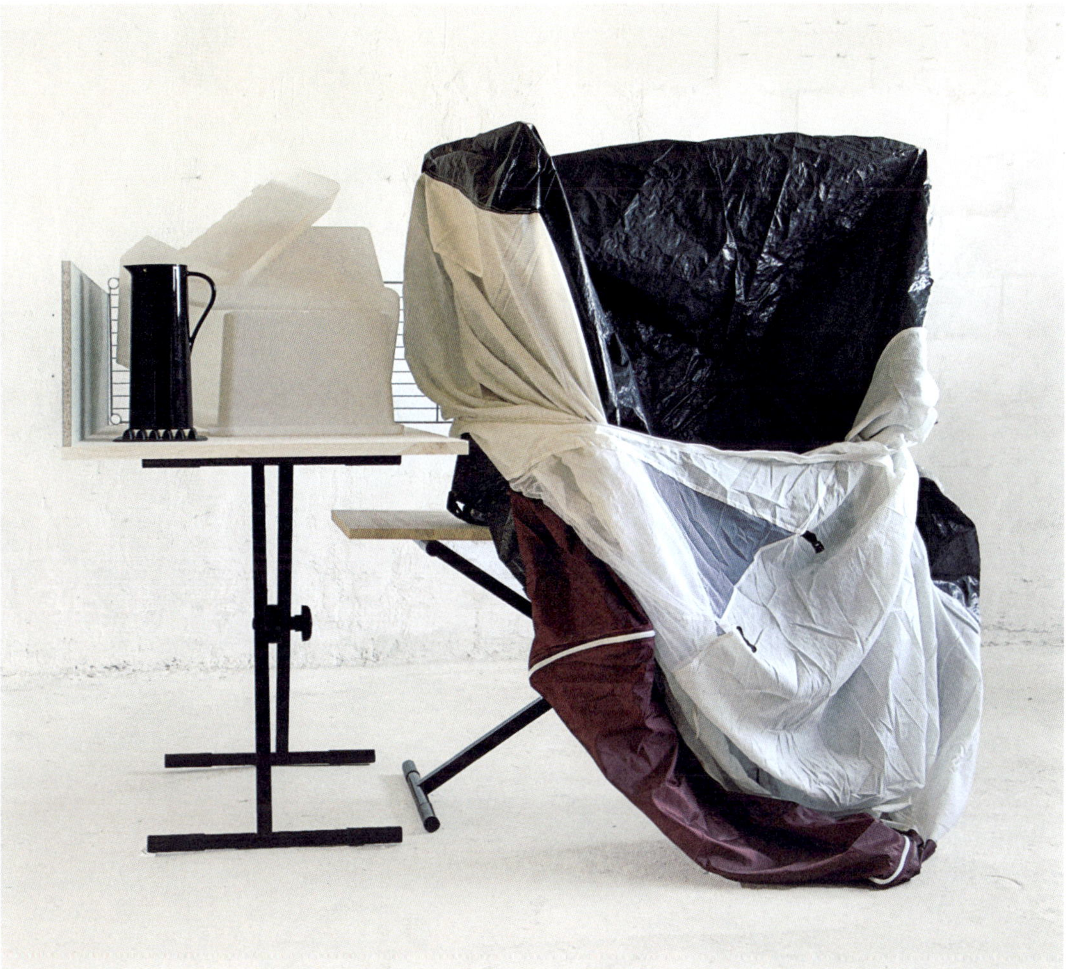

La Caverna
Installation
140 x 180 x 120 cm
2010

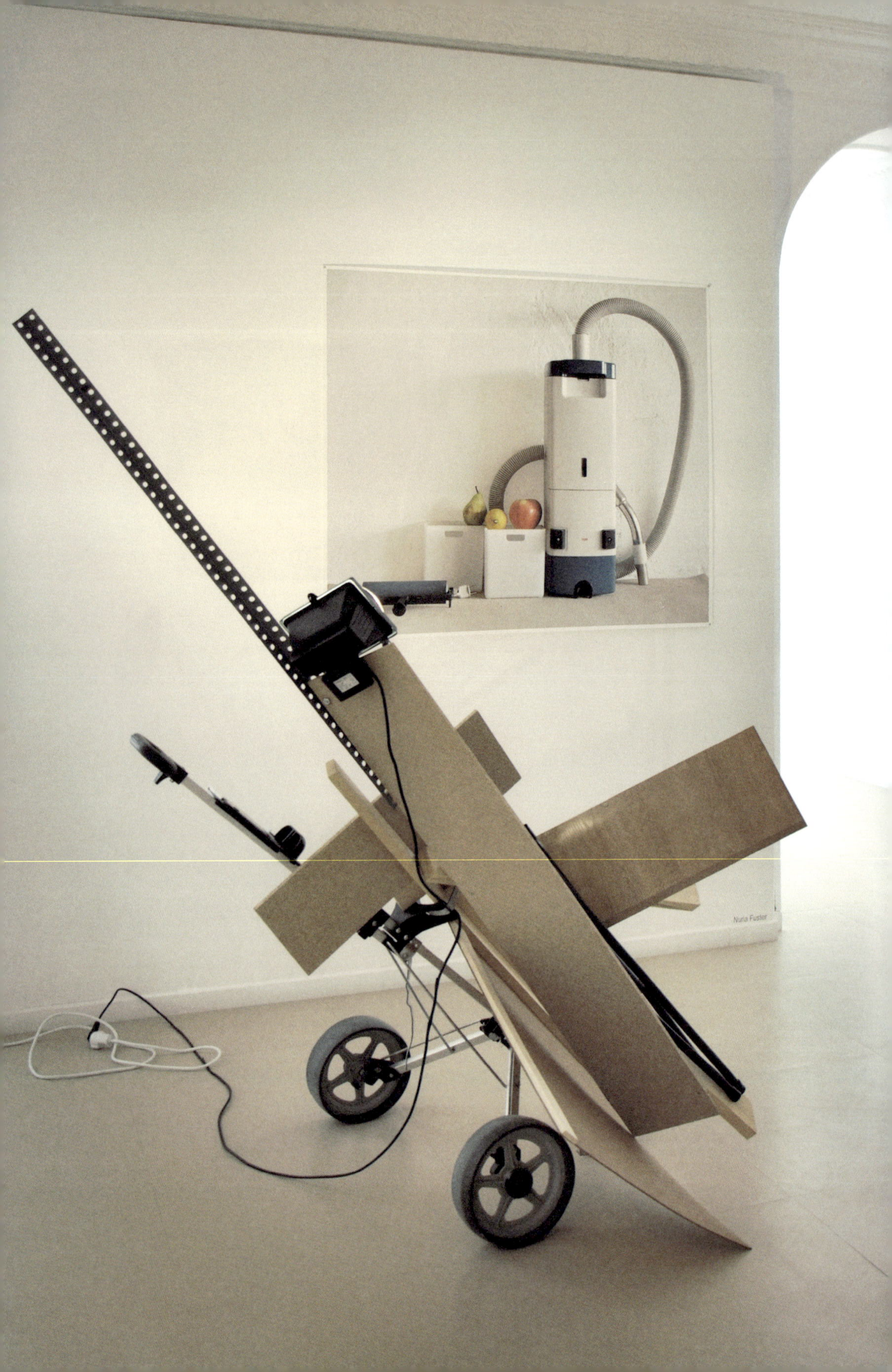
Nuria Fuster

Eagle Rock

Behind the vivarium glass
the reptiles
unmoving.

A woman hangs up washing
in the silence.
Death is becalmed.

In the depths of the ground
my soul glides
silent as a comet.

Tomas Tranströmer
2003

<
Untitled
Installation
Variable measurements
2010

Santiago Giralda

Using one of the purest pictorial practices in existence today as a starting point, Santiago Giralda has created a whirlwind around which his productive and prolific world is starting to be revealed. The objects represented are real and recognisable and form part of the collective imagination. However, by being included on the canvas they offer their own personality in order to be developed as part of a pictorial whole. "By producing new contexts, I constantly question the functions of images and their insertion in our daily lives", says the artist.

Image alteration processes such as collages or digital techniques have allowed him to extract the images which will appear on his canvases. His working method very much takes into account the fact that the image is conditioned by the way in which it is displayed, and therefore uses very direct and colouristic figuration which is always full of chaos and movement.

With an interest in representation and alteration, Santiago Giralda sees the canvas as a force field with which he maintains a dialogue and in which he constructs personal scenarios that are all his own.

María de Corral

Statement

The works presented differ from my previous works due to the irruption of the landscape and the gradual abandonment of interiors and architectural spaces. Through this set of paintings I aim to reconsider the concept of landscape as a construct, which is currently built through the use of media images. The paintings presented refer to imaginary and evocative landscapes which are designed using pre-existing images. I am interested in the relationship established between pictorial tradition and new technologies in the representation and contemplation of a world which would seem to be becoming gradually more digitised. In this context, my works propose the establishment of a space where, using painting as a starting point, we can reflect on the different ways in which we connect with an environment which is increasingly dependent on the means or mechanism by which it is revealed to us.

Santiago Giralda

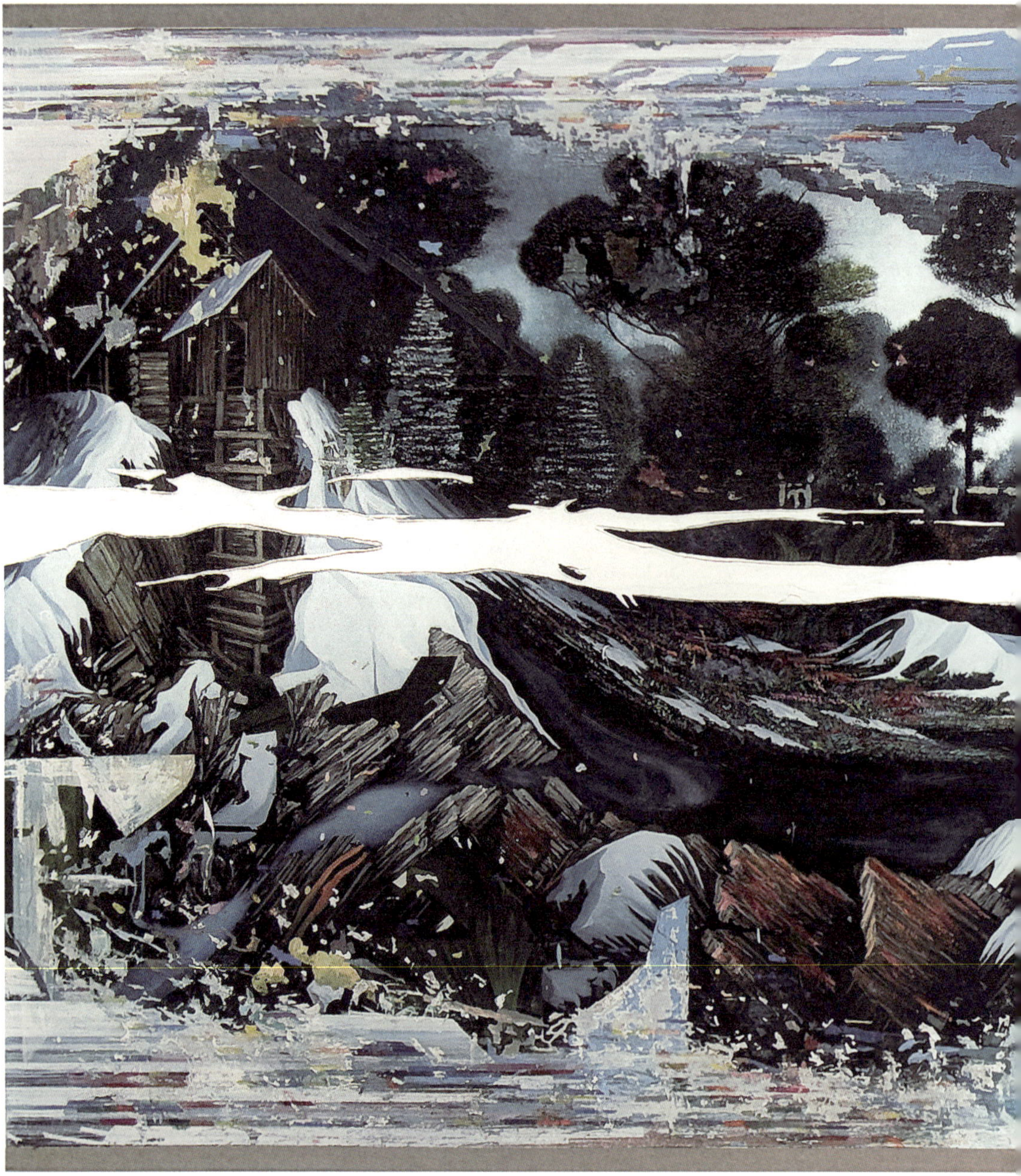

Interface I
Oil on canvas, diptych
180 x 195 cm each
2011

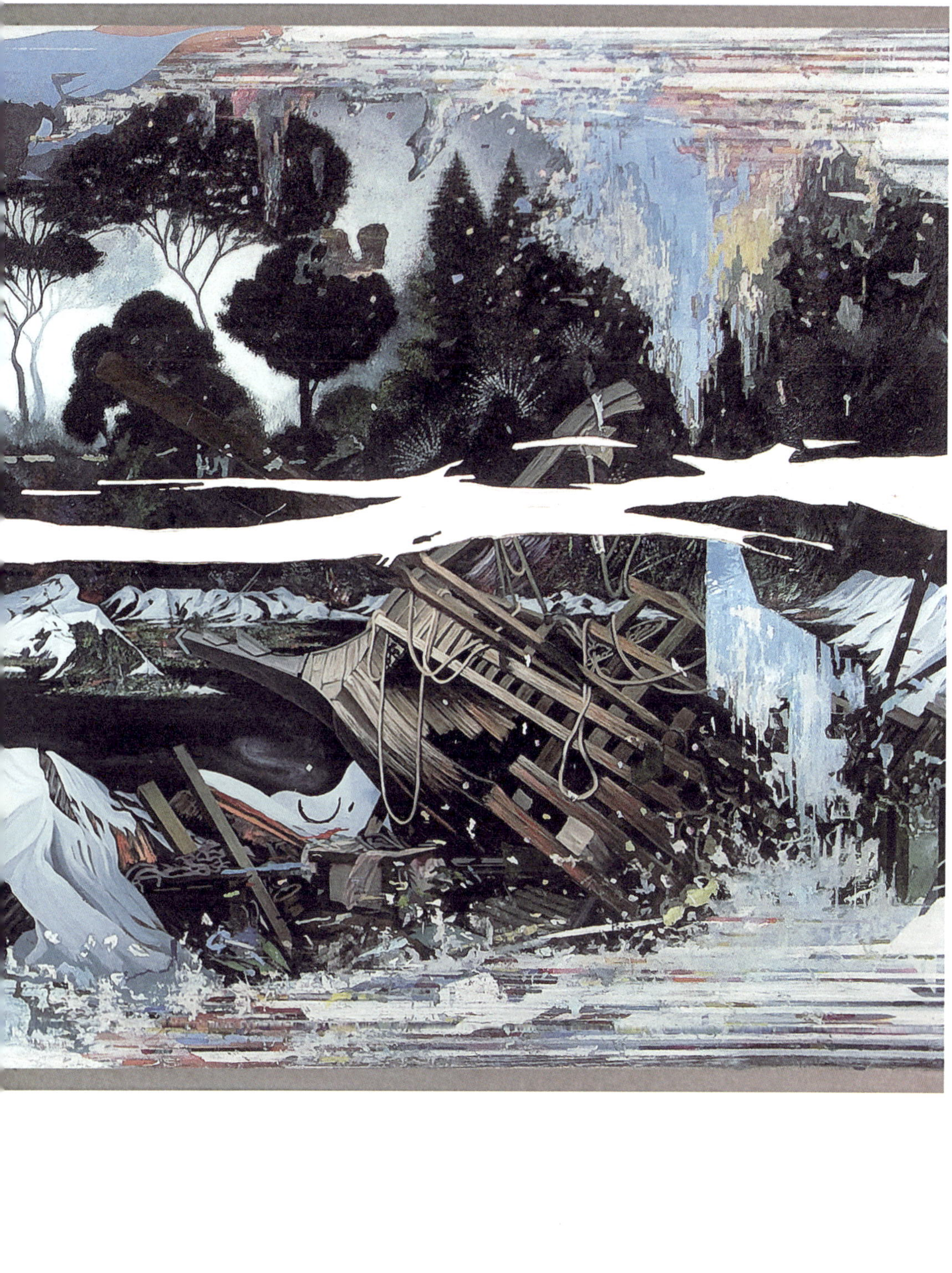

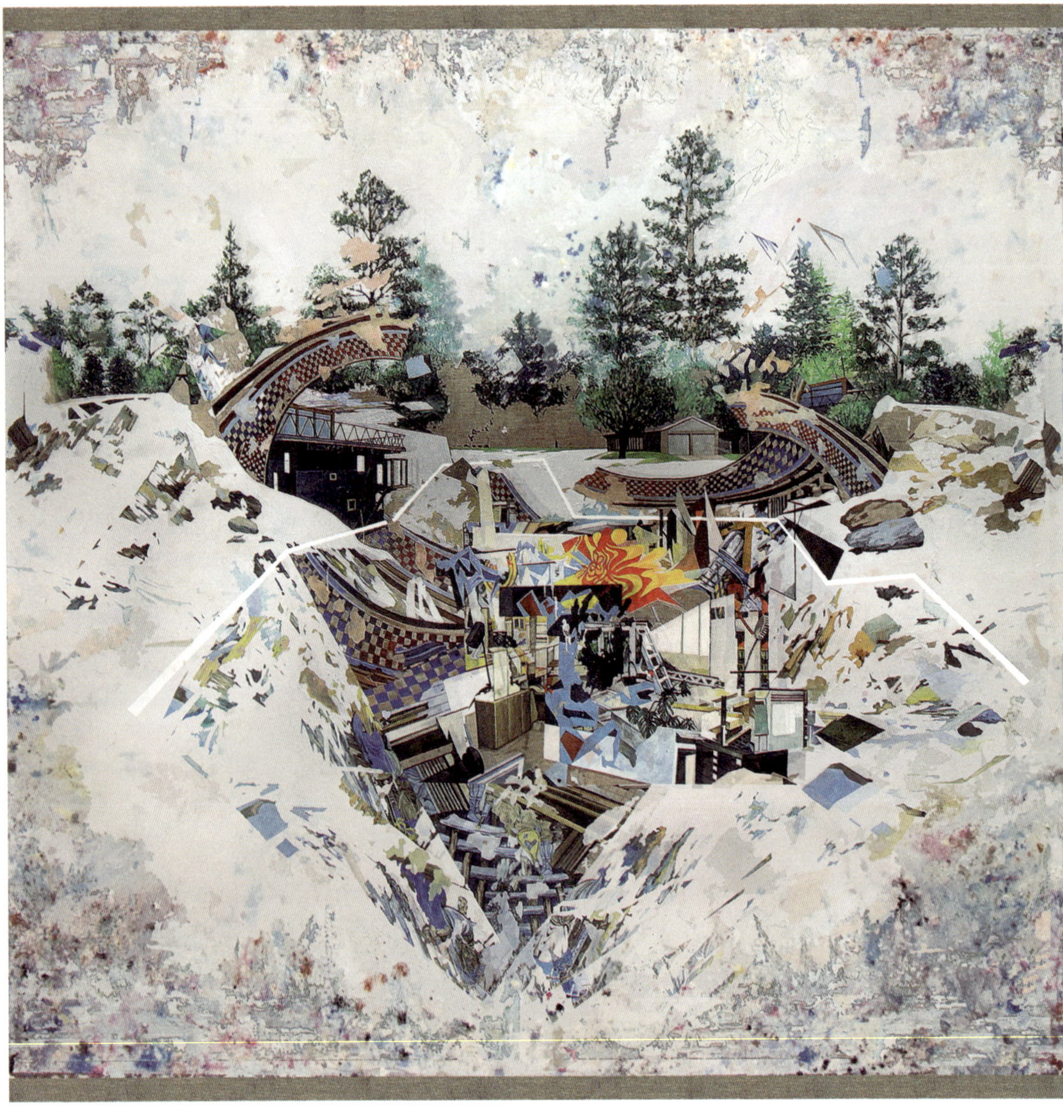

The Bridge
Oil on canvas
195 x 195 cm
2012

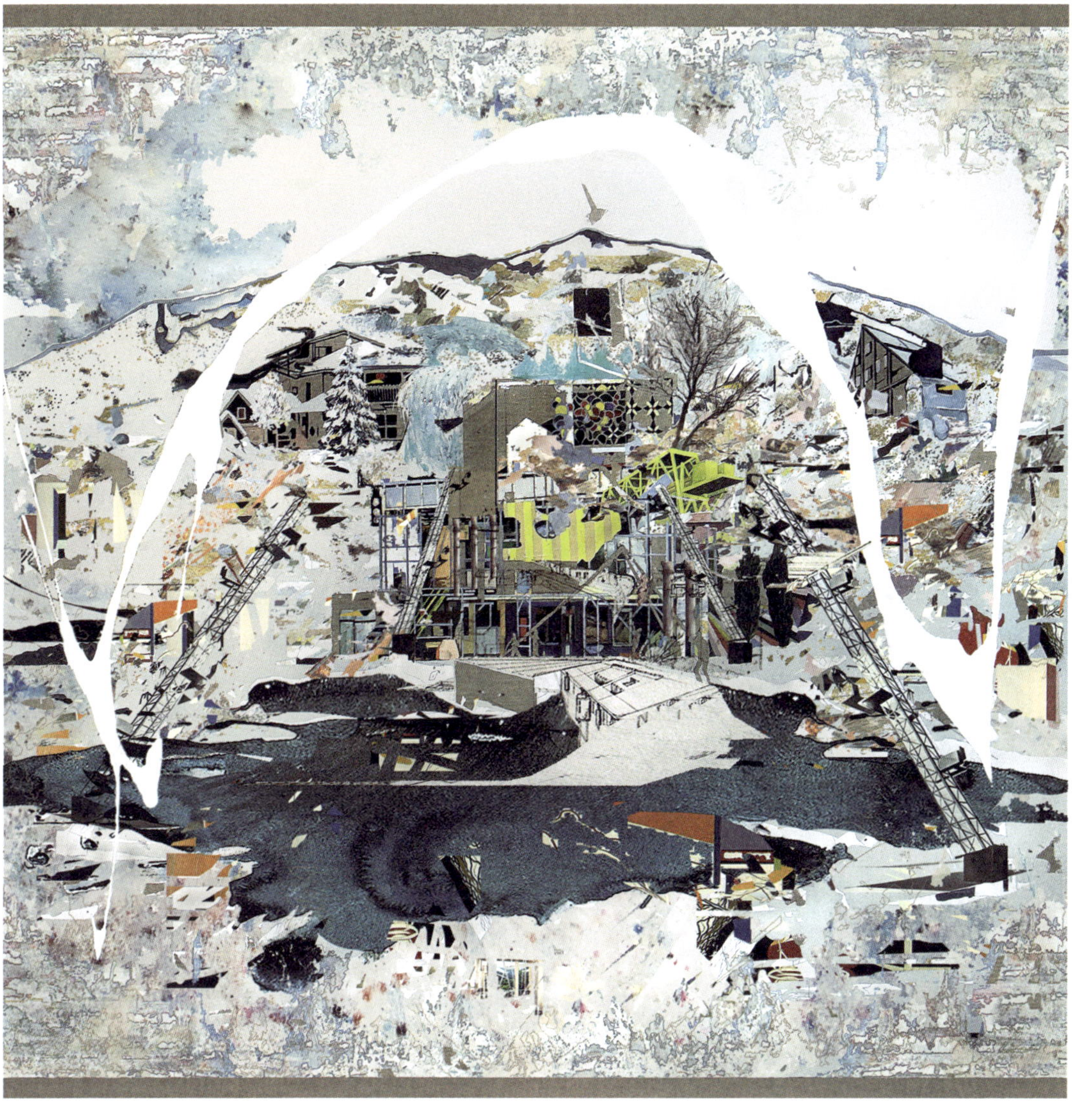

Lago
Oil on canvas
195 x 195 cm
2012

Project

My project considers the contribution that painting has made in the technological and media-influenced context of the knowledge society. New technologies mean that knowledge management is increasingly dependent on image. New equations have thus emerged between knowledge and vision, between mechanism and image, and between reality and representation. This proposal studies the capacity of pictorial images to be perceived not only as representations, but also as links which are able to connect, reconfigure and establish new imaginary scenarios.

Based on pictorial practice, my works bring together different collective imaginations. By producing new contexts from a pictorial perspective, the functions of images and their insertion in our daily lives are constantly questioned. My work offers a particular arrangement of the different objects represented, both real and imagined, which reveals a subjective experience of the pictorial space.

I have depicted spaces which use images of elements with different origins. Some have been taken by me, from my environment, others are fictitious or accidental and have been introduced during the pictorial process, and some are appropriations belonging to other fields. I have experimented on the computer with the possibilities offered by editing and digital image alteration programs, distorting and recomposing the original images through a postproduction process in order to subsequently reconstruct them through painting. What finally happens on the canvas, in terms of the process, can only be simulated with digital tools up to a certain point. Painting entails a number of characteristics in relation to time, anachronism, carnality and meta-story which I believe are fundamental when considering the project.

The functional or referential aspect of the objects (motifs) depicted does not interest me as much as their pictorial potential when composing and creating paths through the pictorial space. The different origins of the images and the wide range of predisposed simultaneous perspectives offer an apparent effect of totality which is in fact illusory, as in the end they reveal that it is impossible for the space to be perceived as a solid, static and timeless unit.

There is no complete or conclusive information in what is depicted, but rather a process of juxtaposition of fragmented attitudes which are subjectively reorganised according to the following: the particular arrangement used when constructing the image, and the use made by spectators of the connections they establish by looking at the image in order to decode it, based on their own personal interpretation. In short, the painting in this project is not aimed at a particular goal but offers a reflection, based on the painting, on image production and visual perception processes.

My project focuses on these types of processes against other representative aspects. It is not a representation or documentation of an external reality, but the construction of my own pictorial reality whose intention is to interconnect with the viewing habits of spectators today and the way in which painting is being redefined in the knowledge society.

Santiago Giralda

Jaime de la Jara

Is it we who speak through words or do words speak through us? One of the distinguishing characteristics of certain kinds of contemporary art lies in the criticism of the picture. This type of art is based on the conviction that there is nothing natural in language, nor is there anything external to it, since it is through language that we understand the world and it is the vehicle by which others relate to us and we to them. But this representation is not neutral: it is immersed in a power structure... and what is more, it strives to achieve power.

It is precisely in the hidden recesses of the picture where the work of Jaime de la Jara is displayed. Through a decontextualisation of images and objects, fragmented at times, he reveals exactly how far appearances can deceive. Nothing is what it seems. So what from a distance appears to be a boat, becomes when seen up close a structure made of felt, clearly incompatible with its function: on contact with the water the textile would no longer fulfil its given purpose of remaining afloat on that water. Like Magritte, Jara considers that all representation is an artifice and he bases himself on the agreed acceptance, and not on the nature of things. On the contrary, very often the material of the object contradicts the apparent function of the image. I believe that one of the novelties in the work of this Madrid artist lies in his use of materials. They are not merely receptors of form, but serve as an independent element in the process of representation and in the construction of the images. They do not answer to an idealised logic external to themselves but are in opposition to that logic of representation, revealing just how artificial it is, how intrinsically violent. In such works as *Spanish boat* we see that De la Jara does not seek so much to reflect the social situation that causes the great number of illegal immigrant vessels in certain areas along the Spanish coast, but rather to criticise a representational system that legitimises objects. The viewer becomes disorientated; in his works the artist succeeds not only in reflecting and criticising certain particular social structures, but also the language in which these are grounded. Nothing is what it seems.

Yolanda Romero

Spanish boat
Synthetic felt, wood and plastic
300 x 130 x 90 cm
2011

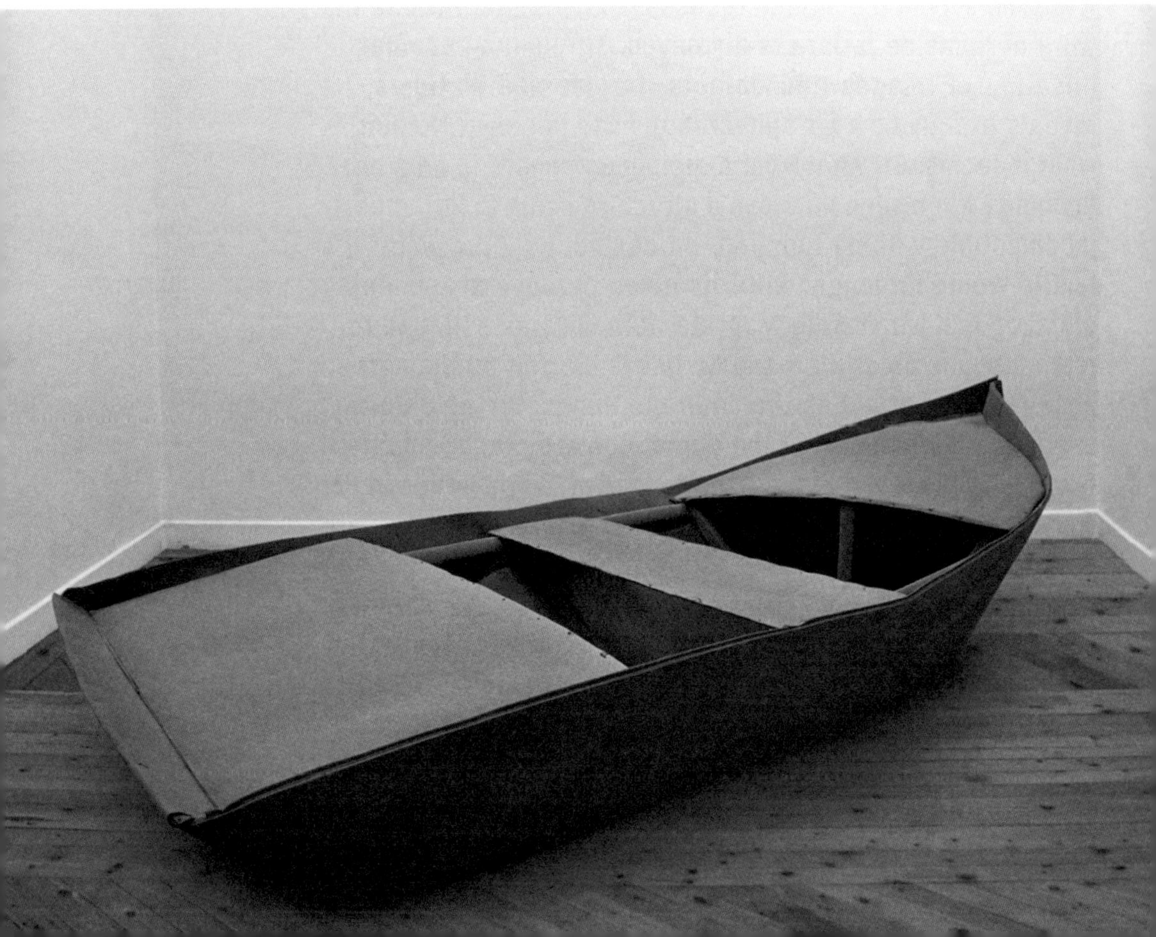

Today I made the ascent of the highest mountain in this region, which is not improperly called Ventosum. My only motive was the wish to see what so great an elevation had to offer. I have had the expedition in mind for many years; for, as you know, I have lived in this region from infancy, having been cast here by that fate which determines the affairs of men. Consequently the mountain, which is visible from a great distance, was ever before my eyes.

Francesco Petrarca, «Letter to Dionisio da Borgo San Sepolcro», *Familiar Letters,* IV, 1.

I see art as a process in which an infinity of tools can be used and dropped – hence art as something that has no limits. Among this infinite number of strategies, I am fascinated by, and constantly employ, the alteration, manipulation and the decontextualisation of reality and its contents. This stems from my enduring interest in discovering how far we can go in knowing our own closest and most fundamental reality, what we apparently we think we know.

Our most direct knowledge is subject to our experience and the rest of our knowledge is determined by it and by other "media". My work plays on these direct media and on these basic resources which give us the possibility of extending our knowledge of things that we cannot experience first-hand. The resources are there to recreate and generate experiences so as to create a very specific focus, as are used in the communication media, the theatre or any other forms of artistic expression. There are a few very clear strategies. As with strategies for the theatre of the absurd to which I constantly refer, there are strategies that deal with the limits of rationality, emphasising the irrational in order to emphasise what is "normal" and attribute greater importance to it.

There is something I always refer to when I have to talk about my work in simple and general terms, in order to point the way to a clearer understanding of my art. I quote what Michael Hardt wrote in his essay *Prison Time*, words that that I have adopted as part of my personal canon, as they are an excellent expression of my permanent intention and of what I set out to achieve in a great deal of my work. Hart maintains that "we have to construct a way that the moment of 'love' will return, that it will repeat incessantly to mark a temporal density, a duration that will be the material structure of a new time". To make time stand still and to reveal not only what generates seemingly "important" changes, but also what does not seem to be important and which, by changing its temporal density through the power of slowness, we may see in a different way. To paraphrase Genet, "someone may have achieved it, albeit in the fraction of a second".

Things are not what they seem; they are much more complex or contain more details and interpretations than can be perceived at first glance.

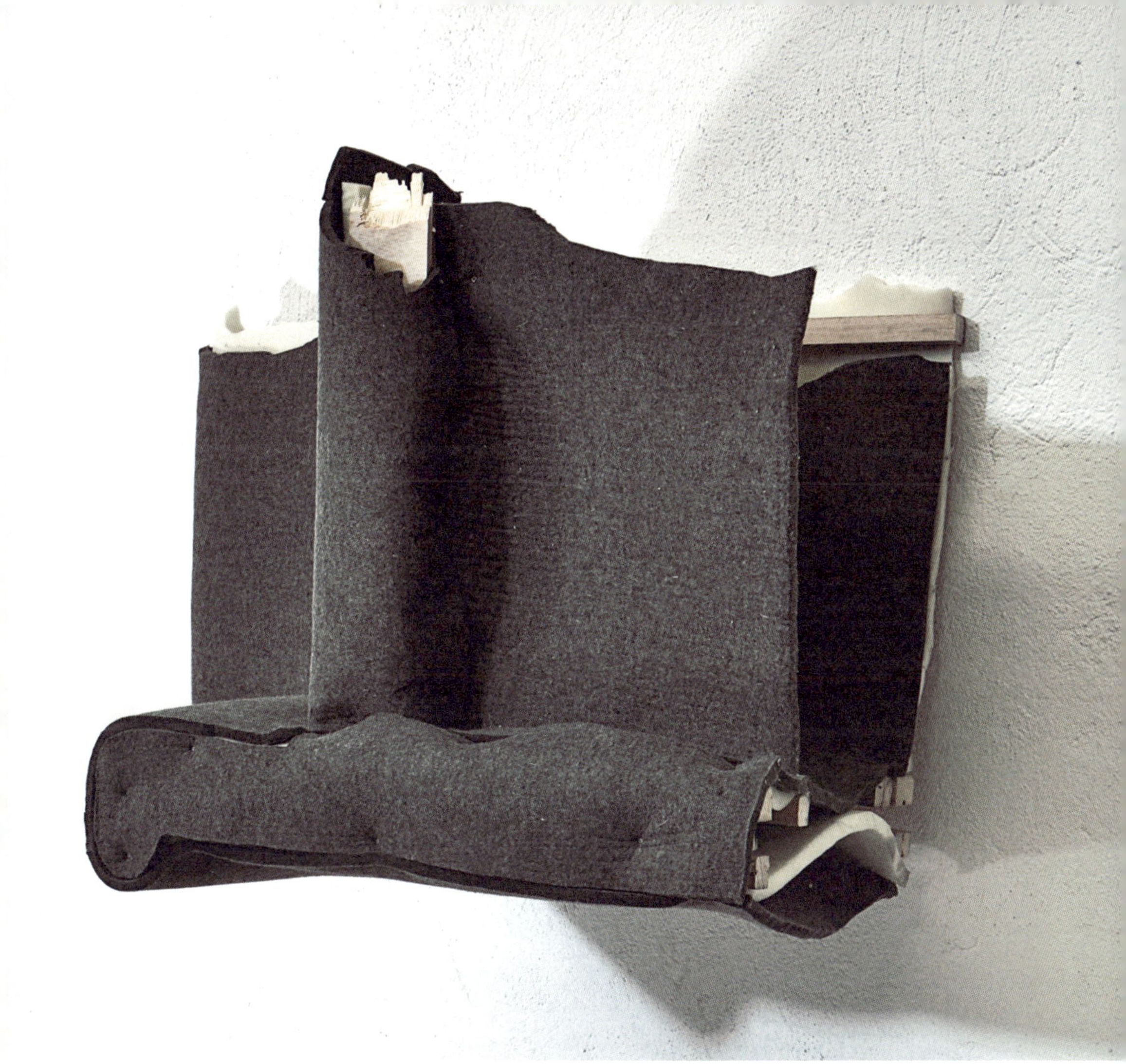

Last_site
Wool felt, synthetic foam and wood
120 x 70 x 75 cm
2011

In the words of Frank Stella: "Things are never as simple as they seem..." Although for some people they are. Reality is fragile and ever-changing. Any change in a single detail can violate it and change a scene into something very different. We form part of that scene, of this reality, making us just as fragile and ever-changing. We are a reflection of what is happening around us.

Jaime de la Jara

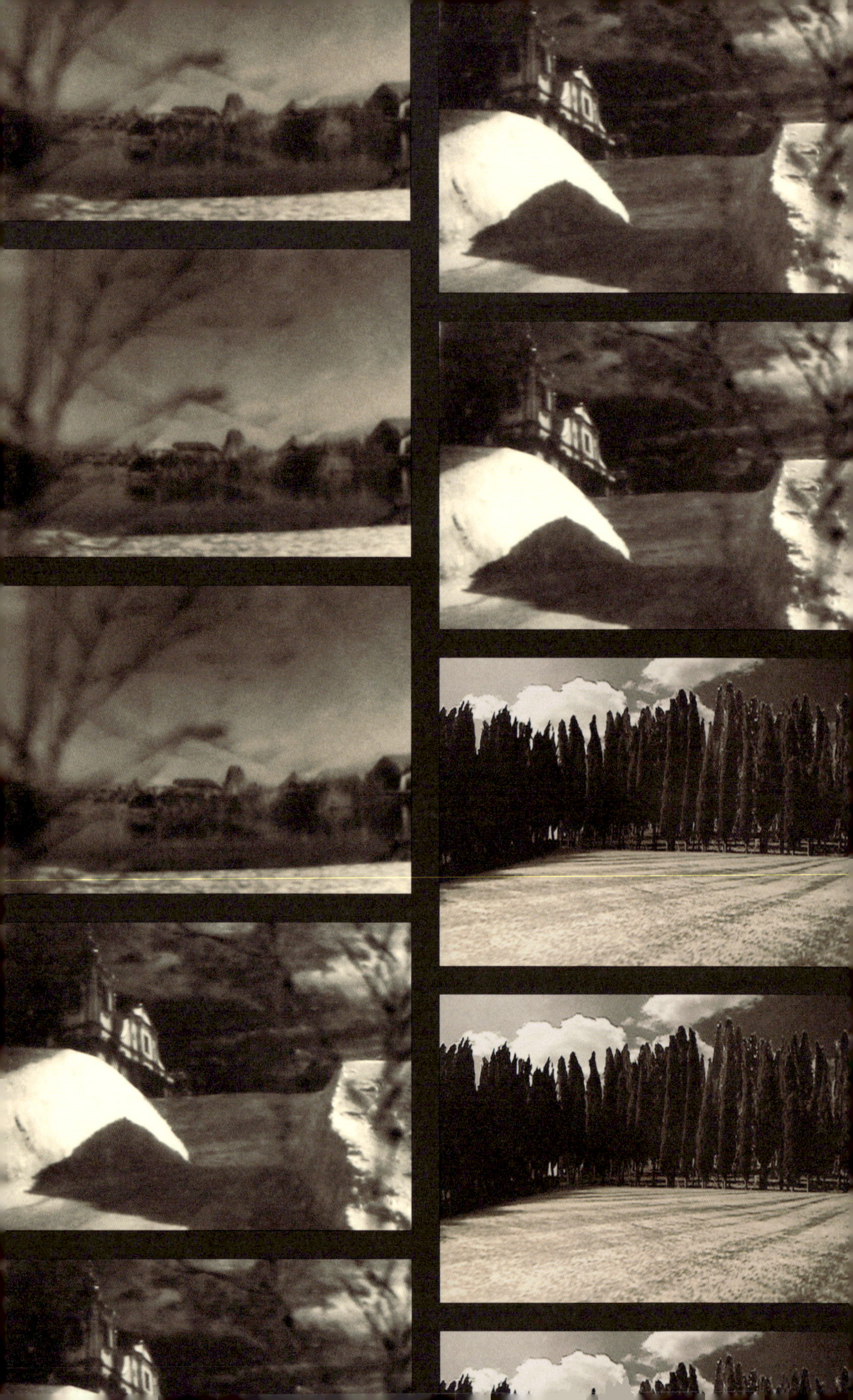

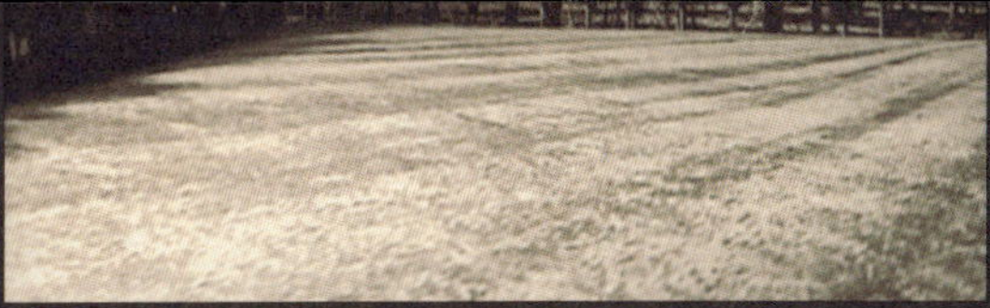

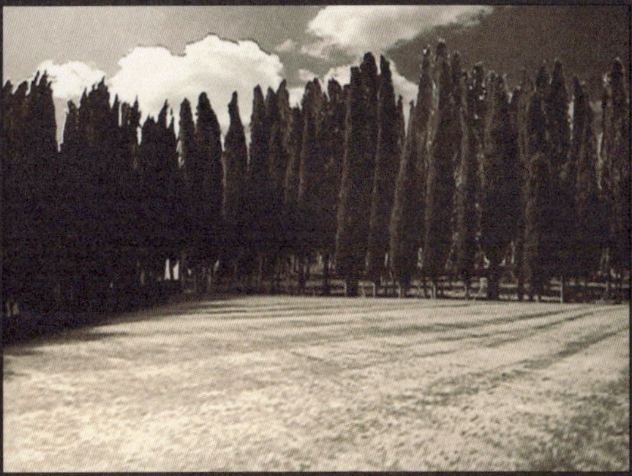

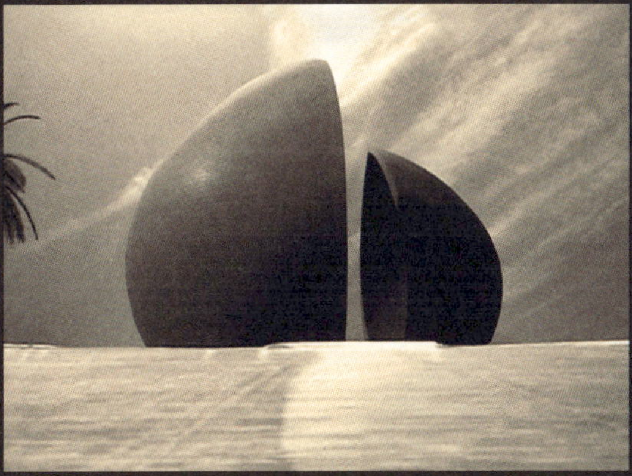

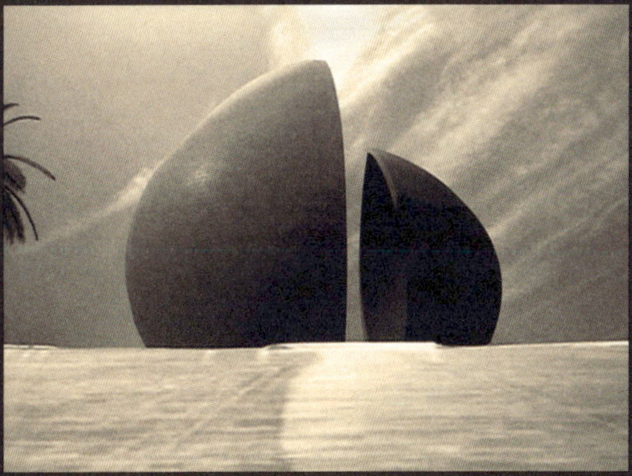

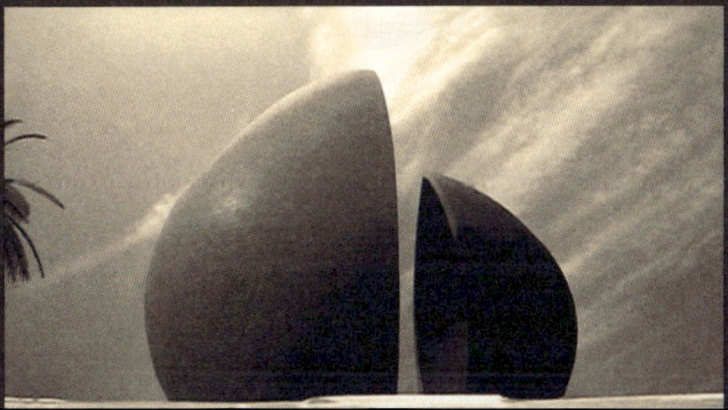

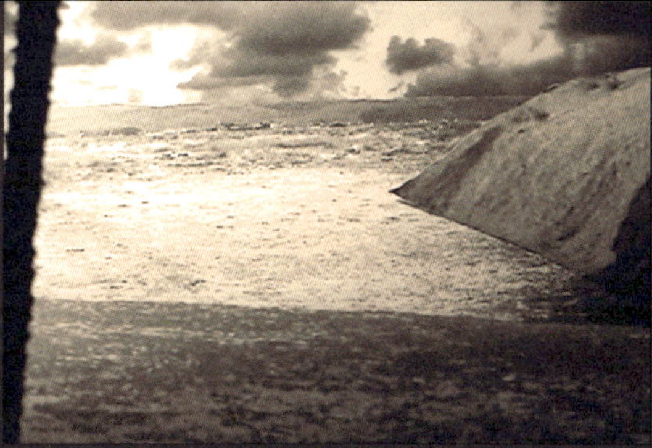

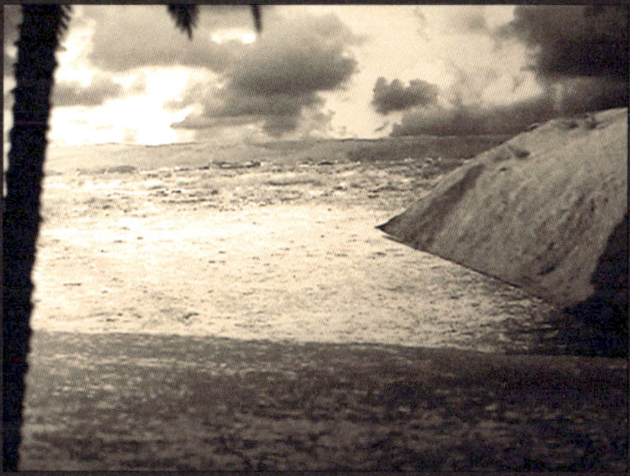

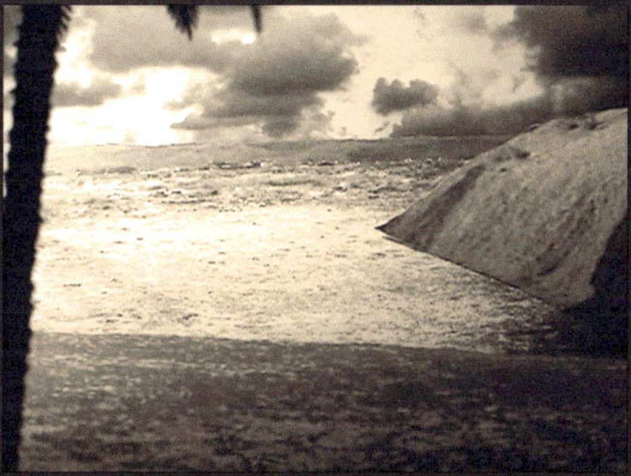

Nowhere
Looped video projection
Master MiniDV
2010/2011

Delving into the environment

Jaime de la Jara, of no particular profession, as contemporary artists should properly be described, has come to our attention as a collector of salvage; basically, an antiquarian who loves what no longer has meaning, even though this includes life experiences that draw our attention to things that do not merit the slightest interest in this digitalised era because of their obsolescence and lack of utility. Let us assume that rationalism took account of the fact that the Vitruvian principle of utility lay within the cold rectangularity of constructivism, which De la Jara considers as exactly the most suitable medium for the perceptive comprehension of his creative work. If this had already been thought in relation to plastic rationalism, what must we of the technological age now think as we prepare to venture into the world of virtual reality? But De la Jara is an artist, and this entails certain determining factors that allow him to regard as relics those obsolete objects that have still survived in our dreary machine-driven reality. It is obvious that his modernity means that he is a person who in his work makes use of the effective tools at man's disposal, without needing to resort to plays on the supposed hidden effectiveness that we attribute to objects that have fallen into disuse.

In the works of De la Jara we are given the impression that we are witnessing the final death rattle of our sensitivity overcome by the effective social realities of technology. And this despite the fact that the artist achieves these results through full and ironic manipulation of a few aspects of a real life that has passed into history. Indeed, he has set down roots in this strange new sensitivity that enjoys the privilege of the advances permitted by the current media, without for all that relinquishing the underlying sentimental archaisms – for this is what we experience when presented with his work.

Sentimental resources

His resources are: the "installation" – occupation of the space in order to restore a taste for the archaic –; continuous "sequential projection" – the dense presence, through movement, of a notion of lost time, but nonetheless, of chronology –; the "exhibition" effect – so that we are aware that we are not witnessing the reality of what we actually perceive – and (in an attempt to reduce the distancing between the real and the virtual) a relentless, but not unsettling, "sound" effect that situates the receiver in the reality of the setting in which the creative action of the artist takes place. The observer's senses become lost in a type of endless loop between real object and manipulated object. Which is the reality and which the manipulation? De la Jara tears down icons; he presents them as objects of false perception. Behind all this gratifying and disturbing work lies a wicked and calculated intention to destroy. Objective reality is modified until it becomes absurd desire for what can never be achieved.

Arnau Puig
Review of the exhibition
in the Palma Dotze Gallery,
Vilafranca del Penedès,
Barcelona (2004)

The truth of lies

If we paid greater attention to our viewing point and the conditions in which we view, we wouldn't make the mistake of believing that our senses deceive us. Jaime de la Jara decided to undertake the task of giving expression to his opinions on the subject. To do this he situated himself within the suggestive and deceitful reality of objects, their narratives and their perception. He realised that the structure of truth and lies arises from beliefs and not from reality: that beliefs are what count, and that if the light from a window is brighter or darker, if it broadens or lengthens or is reduced or attenuated, the reason that explains it must be sought in the conditions and wishes of observation and not in the objects themselves, which are just as we find them or situate them. Mysteries, cadences, incongruities, are projections by the viewer who, if he were situated in other conditions, would produce other views. If we clear away all nostalgic feelings and phantoms regarding the beauty of deceit, with drawings, photos, two-way mirrors, videos, screens, models, sounds, spotlights or structures, the credentials of the current objective are achieved.

Arnau Puig
Review of the exhibition *Lie*
in the Tecla Sala Art Centre,
L'Hospitalet de Llobregat,
Barcelona (2009)

Miki Leal

Miki Leal, who always works with paper, explores a very personal type of abstract figuration with pop and oneiric colouring. Much in the way of fantasies, the scenes that he creates using a refined pictorial technique are imaginings of shapes and colours derived directly from the tribulations of the artist's mind. His working method makes use of association to unearth discoveries that he then elaborates with all the energy, force and versatility that is characteristic of his painting. "I've gone through various creative processes, but it has always been a process particular to the abstract artist, as I always start off with a blank sheet. The important thing is to keep on unravelling the thread until something takes shape that has a reference to what's going on in your head at the time."

The variety of subjects depicted is enormous. It could be said that he gives expression to his entire personal universe through music, cinema, literature, travel or the people closest to him. With an optimism typical of those from Seville, Miki Leal faces up to his job as an artist. He knows that his art is authentic and says so unreservedly. His recent work focuses on landscapes and watercolour, a technique that he masters perfectly, as he has demonstrated on many occasions in his exhibitions in Spain and abroad, while his reputation continues to grow.

María de Corral

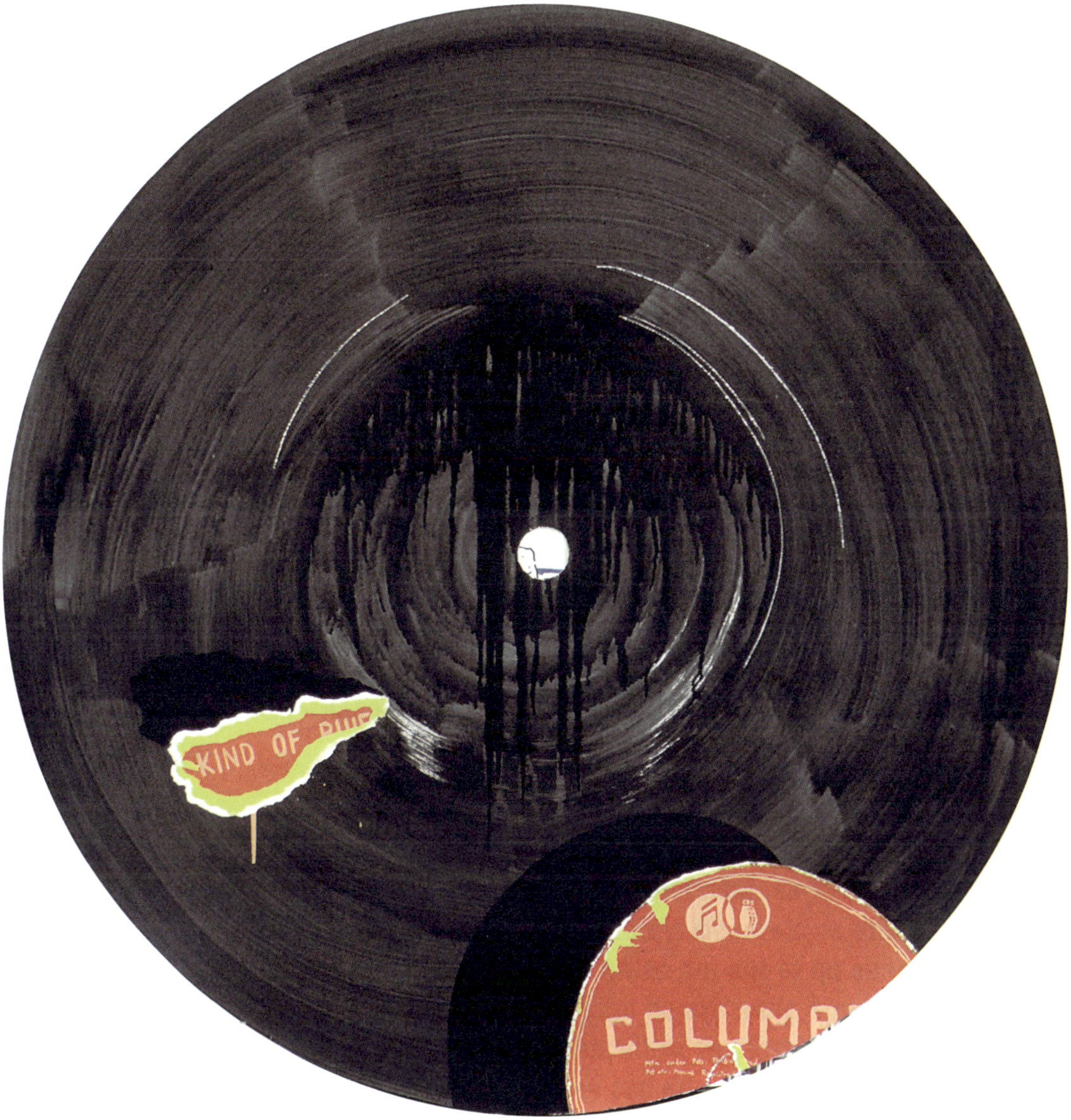

Kind_of_blue
Watercolour and acrylic on paper
Diameter 150 cm
2008

>
The_Bird
Watercolour
and acrylic on paper
150 x 210 cm
2008

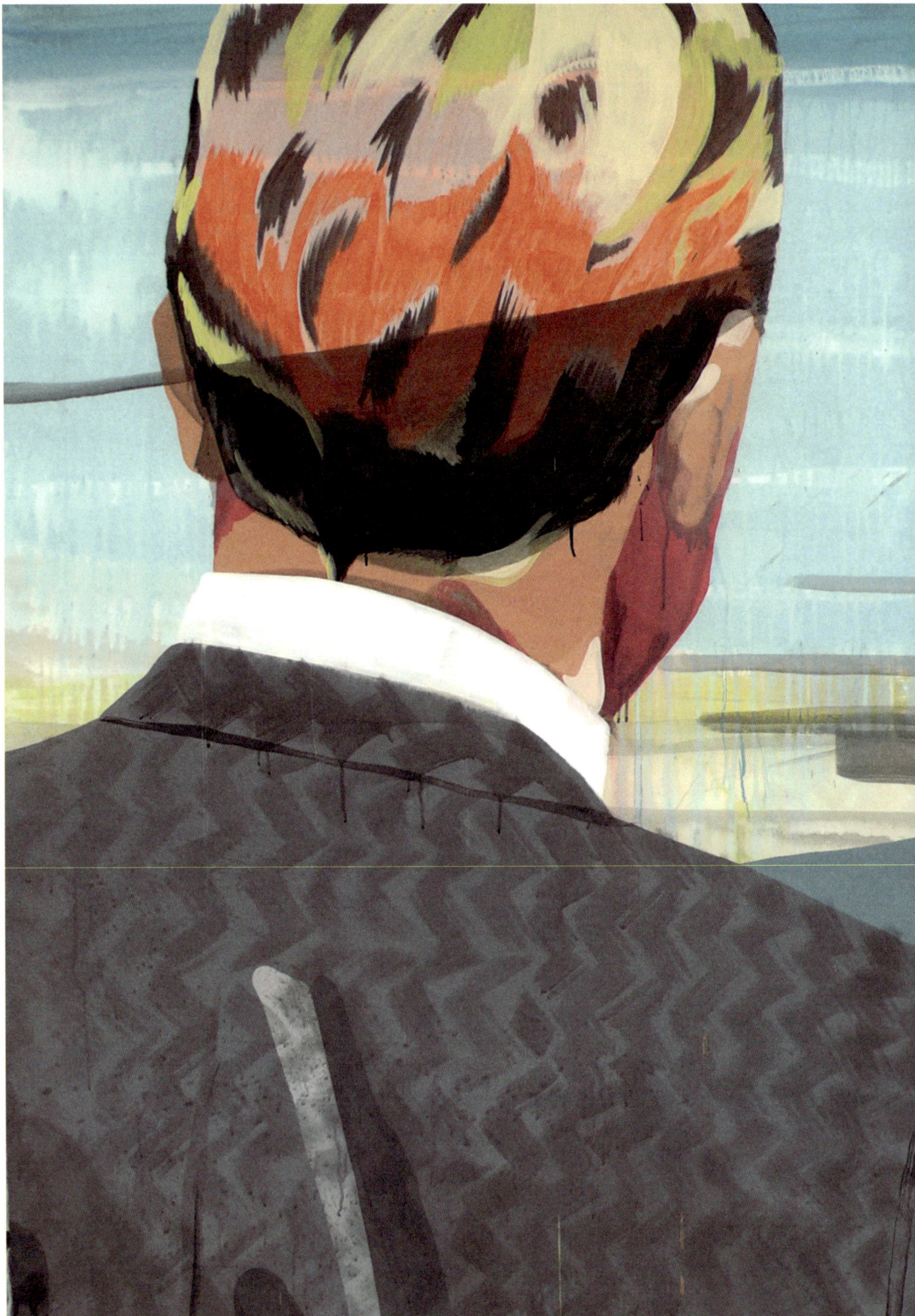

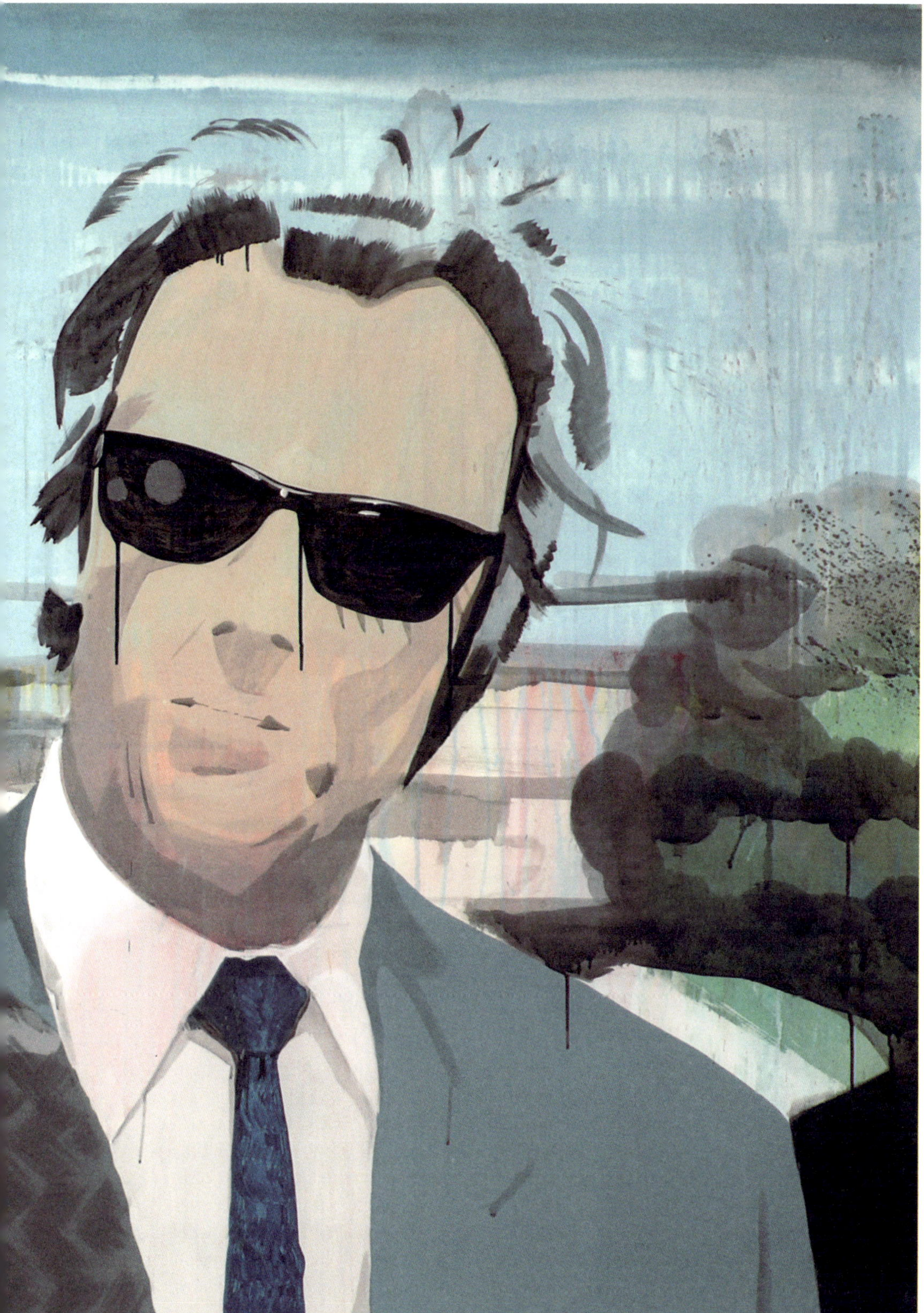

Do you mean that the dialogue says one thing and the image another?
That's a fundamental point in film directing.
It seems to me that in life things often happen like that.

Alfred Hitchcock

I dropped old Phoebe's record. It broke into about fifty pieces [...].
I damn near cried, it made me feel so terrible, but all I did was,
I took the pieces out of the envelope and put them in my coat pocket.
They weren't any good for anything, but I didn't feel like just throwing them away.

J.D. Salinger, *The Catcher in the Rye*

Cinema, jazz, photography or literature, anything that Miki Leal encounters ends up being transformed into pictorial language. When asked, he likes to say (half in jest) that in his work he restricts himself to speaking about himself. And even if he is telling the truth, he is lying, because the world that he perceives is not the world that we see, but rather the one that he absorbs, retains and changes at whim with a creator's unavoidable, selfish freedom.

The works of good artists defy time and "continue to live on like the wristwatches of dead soldiers", in the words of Cocteau, and Miki Leal is a watch thief. In fact all artists are: novelists who violate other people's stories, even the history of mankind itself, in order to "make beautiful creatures from it", and artists who feed off images (in this case cinema) to give expression to their own dreams. Everything is possible and licit. Perhaps this is one reason why the shots selected by Miki Leal are precisely those that no longer tell us anything; ones that

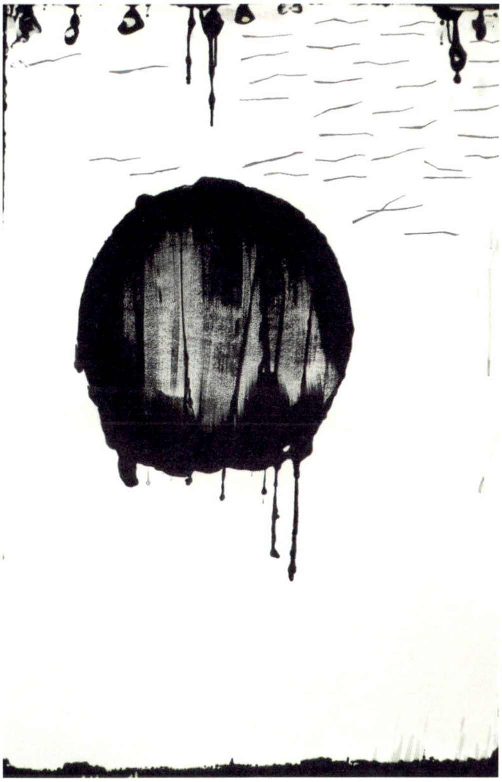

Carátula
Acrylic and pencil on paper
115 x 76 cm.
2008

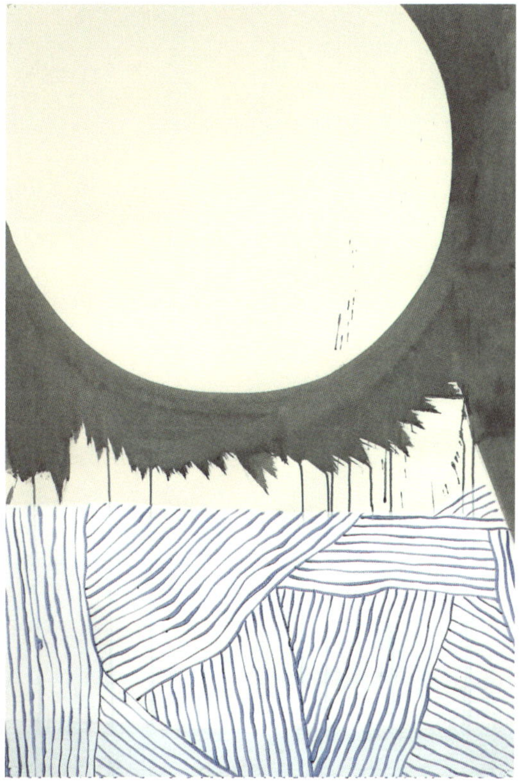

La galleta
Watercolour and acrylic on paper, 115 x 76 cm.
2008

are images pure and simple, nothing more: the image that for a few seconds is a still picture on the screen. There is no narrative intention in them, not even when taken as a whole. This is the key to all of his work: open, profound images that go beyond what that image itself depicts.

Mikitology is the terrain in which Miki Leal paints and lives; from where he looks at other pictures, chooses scenes from films, selects record sleeves or discovers books. *Mikitology* is a personal, cryptic world, which the artist quite innocently forbids anyone to enter, only coming out occasionally for those who approach with interest and curiosity, opening his doors to us like the perfect host as he displays on the floor or hangs on the wall the paper sheets on which the remains of the lives fabricated by Miki Leal have slowly collected.

María José Solano Franco

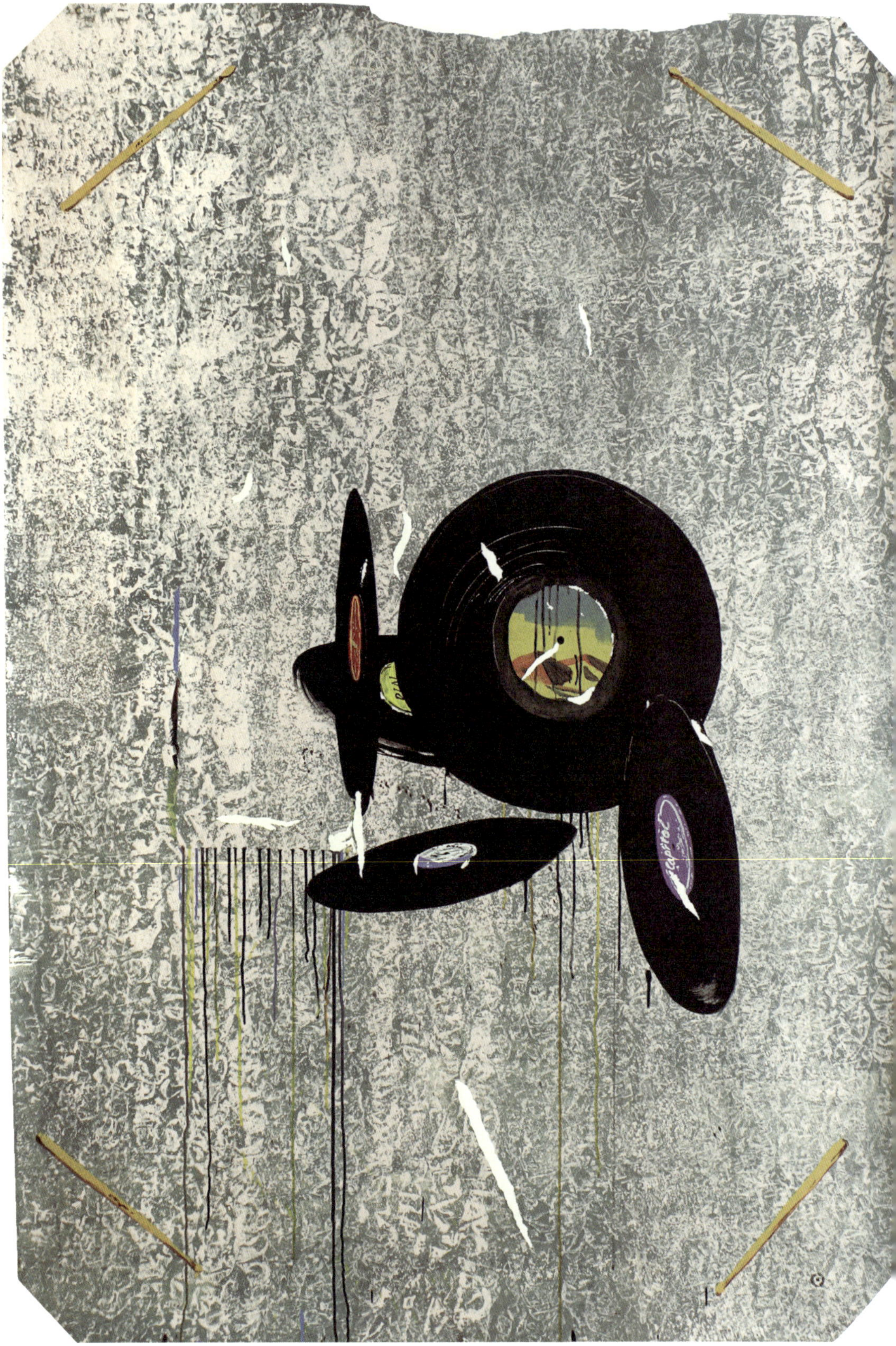

The Red (Sports) Shoes

I was introduced to Miki Leal in the Andalusian Centre for Contemporary Art, in Seville. I was not yet familiar with his work, and I still particularly remember the sports shoes he wore that day, of such a vivid red that when he moved he gave the impression of dancing giddily. Never had I seen trainers in such a bright, dazzling, luscious vermilion... Anyone capable of wearing shoes like that certainly had to be a person very sure of himself, and I loved those shoes so much that I am still envious of the natural way that Miki wore them. Later on I saw some drawings of his, very scant drawings, resembling sketches, in which the forms, figures and patches of colour were arranged on the page without apparent order, with much of the surface left blank, like ideas noted down on sheets of paper as they occurred. But nevertheless, it seemed evident to me that I was looking at the work of a painter. A painter with a sense of colour that turns this into the true main protagonist; it is what predominates and lingers in the memory. When I later mentioned this to him, he told me that he felt he was a painter; that even when he worked with paper, ballpoint pen or ink, he thought of himself as a painter.

Miki Leal's work does not seem to be born impelled by some wish or from the need to provide a response to the previous generation: he takes on board every artistic tradition and may even turn his hand to any he is unfamiliar with; he incorporates any elements that cross his path – or his mind – with complete self-confidence and without having to toe a pre-ordained line. In his most recent exhibition in Madrid, each of the exhibits related a different story whose meaning I did not fully grasp, but in all of them I felt that I perceived that the narration was just another element in the work and that it was not essential to be familiar with it. They seemed to suggest a multitude of references: songs, scenes from television documentaries, from the cinema or the news, or simply invented, they never failed to suggest and recount to me a private world through the paintings. Freshness, lack of inhibition, rhythm and a judicious use of colour are the real subject of those works.

His works appear to be executed somewhat haphazardly, without the slightest pretension to showiness or craftsmanship. Sometimes one of them is painted like a backdrop which, seen up close, becomes implausible and only from distance produces the appropriate effect. Nevertheless, all is achieved without resorting to tricks, artlessly, with freshness, as if the painting emerged fluidly and naturally, without the least effort. There are artists who seem to possess an innate gift, and that is to be admired, since we all know that even the loveliest of voices must be trained before it can make us believe that if flows as if by a miracle. Something similar happens to me when I look at the works of Miki Leal, and I believe that one would not feel uncomfortable to witness a "loss of control", like the Disney character who plays at being a wizard until in the end his powers get out of hand. He certainly has fun playing this role from time to time, demonstrating – albeit with a smile – that the nature of his work is closely linked to his constant questing and his urchin side. Perhaps those red (sports) shoes were enchanted (something I have occasionally considered) and continue to exert their influence even though he no longer wears them. Or maybe it was he who invented the colour of those shoes – with his mastery in the handling of colours.

Ignacio Tovar
2007

<
Bodegón 1
Watercolour and acrylic on paper
200 x 150 cm
2011

Juan López

Juan López mainly focuses on the creation of installations and videos in which there is a clear mix of urban and artistic language. His first works were a series of wall paintings done mostly in insulating tape which set out to change the work place through drawing and ephemeral architecture.

The work of Juan López is filled with references and allusions to the space and urban cultures; they look like advertising hoardings, street furniture or phrases that draw the attention of passers-by. He generally makes use of ephemeral and waste materials, as well as posters, graffiti, placards and stickers, along with other elements: "On walls where concert posters accumulate on top of each other, I do bas-reliefs using a Stanley knife: I cut out phrases and designs, digging out and removing layers and colours", the artist explains. In this way both his installations and his videos attempt to transfer the urban space into the exhibition space, bringing the interior into contact with the exterior.

The intention of the artist is to work on the space in order to change perceptions through tricks of perspective and the use of materials, as in the drawing in insulating tape and the vinyls of photographic images.

María de Corral

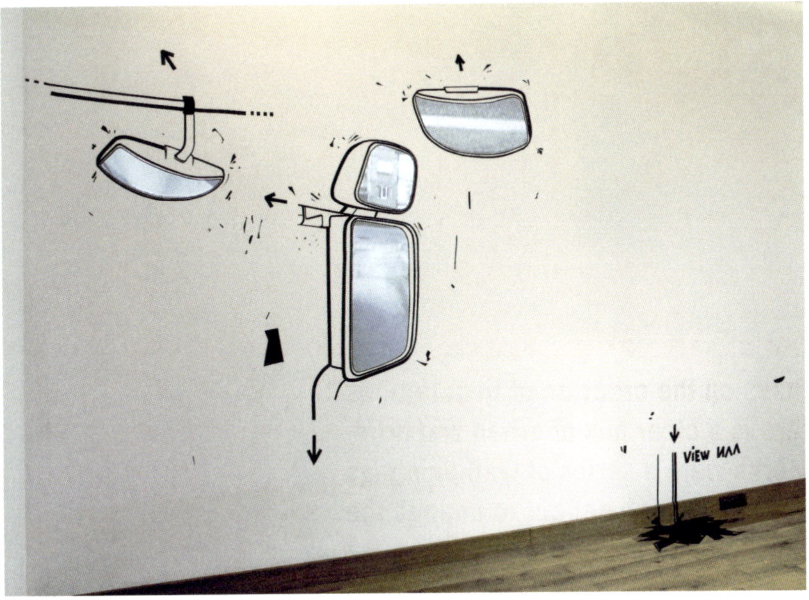

Ill_View
Insulating tape and video projection
Variable measurements
2011

Rear-view mirrors of lorries give us a fleeting view of a particular urban landscape. A quick visit that does not allow us to examine a place in depth.

The work explores the aesthetic possibilities of the urban environment, plays with the space, links video projections with installations and designs complex iconic constructions. Underlying is a profound interest in bringing street-evolved language into direct contact with the different artistic codes typically adopted in the private and institutional domains. These productions are filled with elements that make immediate reference to the urban space.

Juan López

Drawing and removals

Imagine a swimming pool: and if we took away the swimming pool and drew its absent shape in adhesive tape, what chances would we have of charging an entrance fee of 4 euros? How does the newly-arrived audience interact with a newly-created public space? Using the little ladder, queuing in single file to dip into the meanings? They would rather, and I mean much rather, take their breakfast on the lawn in comfort; happy that the uncomfortable stairs, possible barriers, and street manners, have disappeared; and they would get out the good wine to toast the new hydrographic plan. All this because of nothing, for having got rid of the hard-to-digest weight of the sculpture's medium, cold-shouldering the double-crossing VHS and posting a few nice slogans, as easy or as hard as chewing-gum.

But no monument worth its salt has ever wriggled free from the support of its support. And does not do so here. The mere knowledge of its relocation would turn *Balzac* into the MGM lion, and no harm need to come to anyone. A poetic emerges in removals caused by the spatial dyslexia that stems from moving things from one place to another; and it is in that critical state that you come to know the infrastructure of a space. This knowledge can then be applied subsequently to improve or disimprove that space. The same thing, but in drawing.

Pieces that bounce and land in a new place, bringing death to the walls and floor. Furniture that serve for a while, that relinquishes its decorative virtues and designs to the speculation of art. Sculptures fresher than a lettuce.

Drawings more intelligent than the drawer, they are astonished to see others' faces viewing them from such proximity, and recite their silly verses so close that their whispers deceive the guard, who leaves open the doors exhibition hall, so that the mother of the venue enters with the draught that changes the swimming pool into song, and the venue snorts little bleats of heartbreak and nostalgia from other floors.

With the change of bed
The noise ceases to disturb.

My ears mould their form
to the new pillow,
and sleep attempts to find a place
before the next alert.

José Julián Soánez
(Text for the catalogue
of the exhibition *Urbania*, 2003)

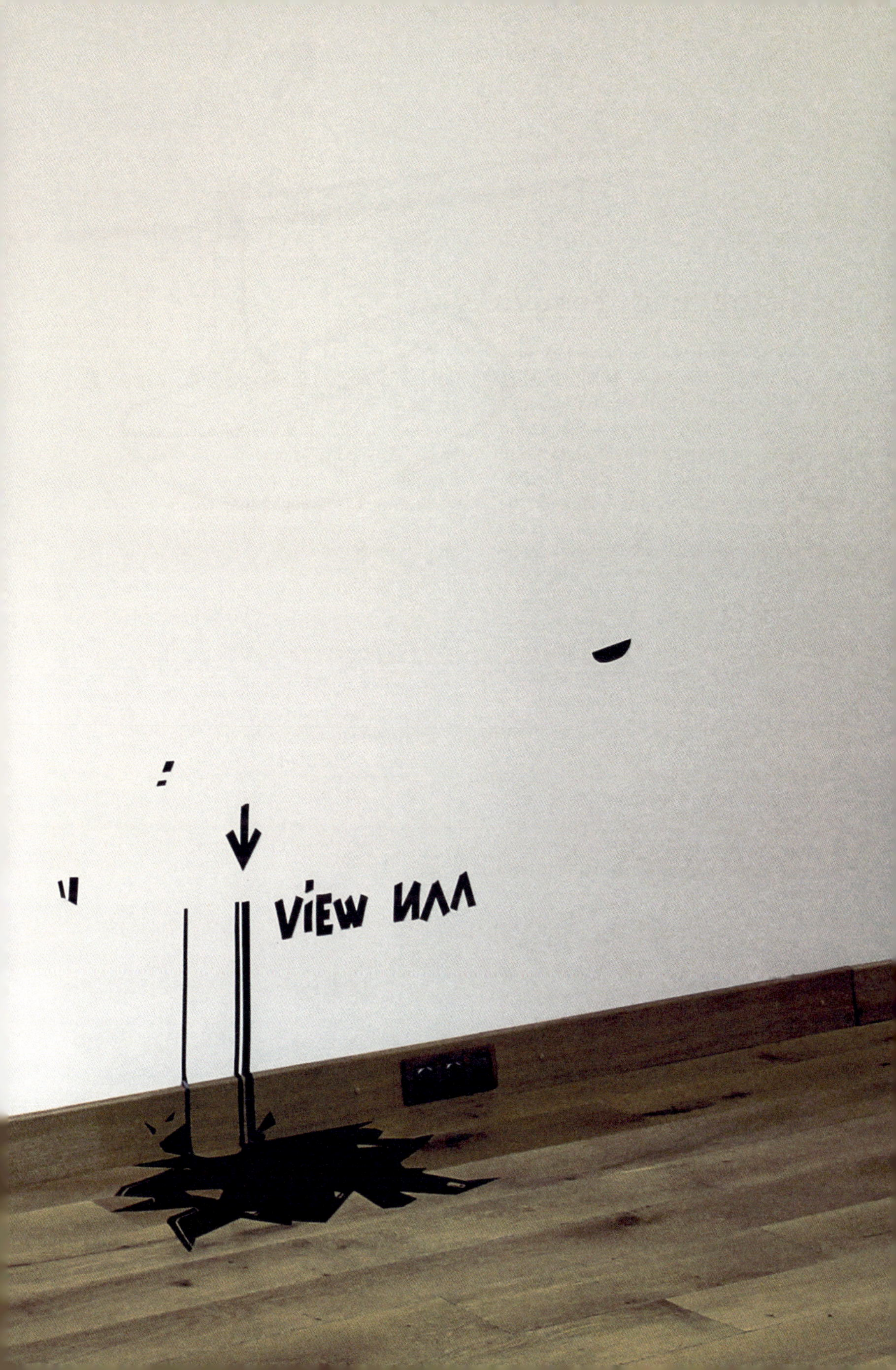
VIEW

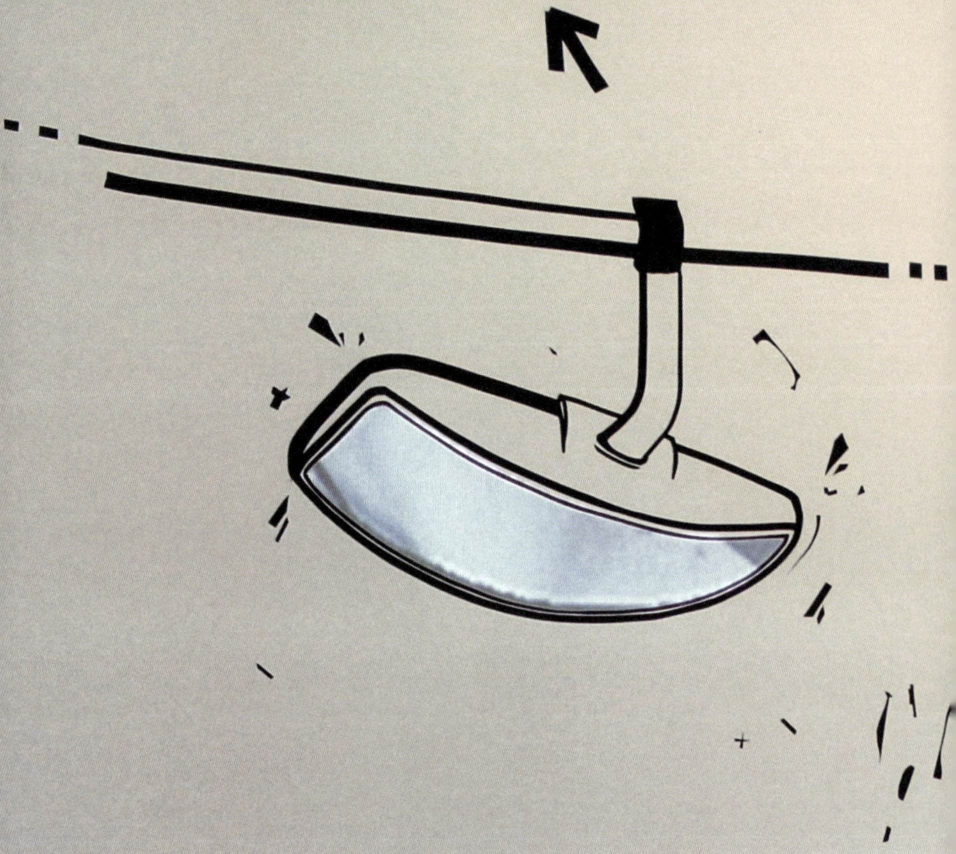

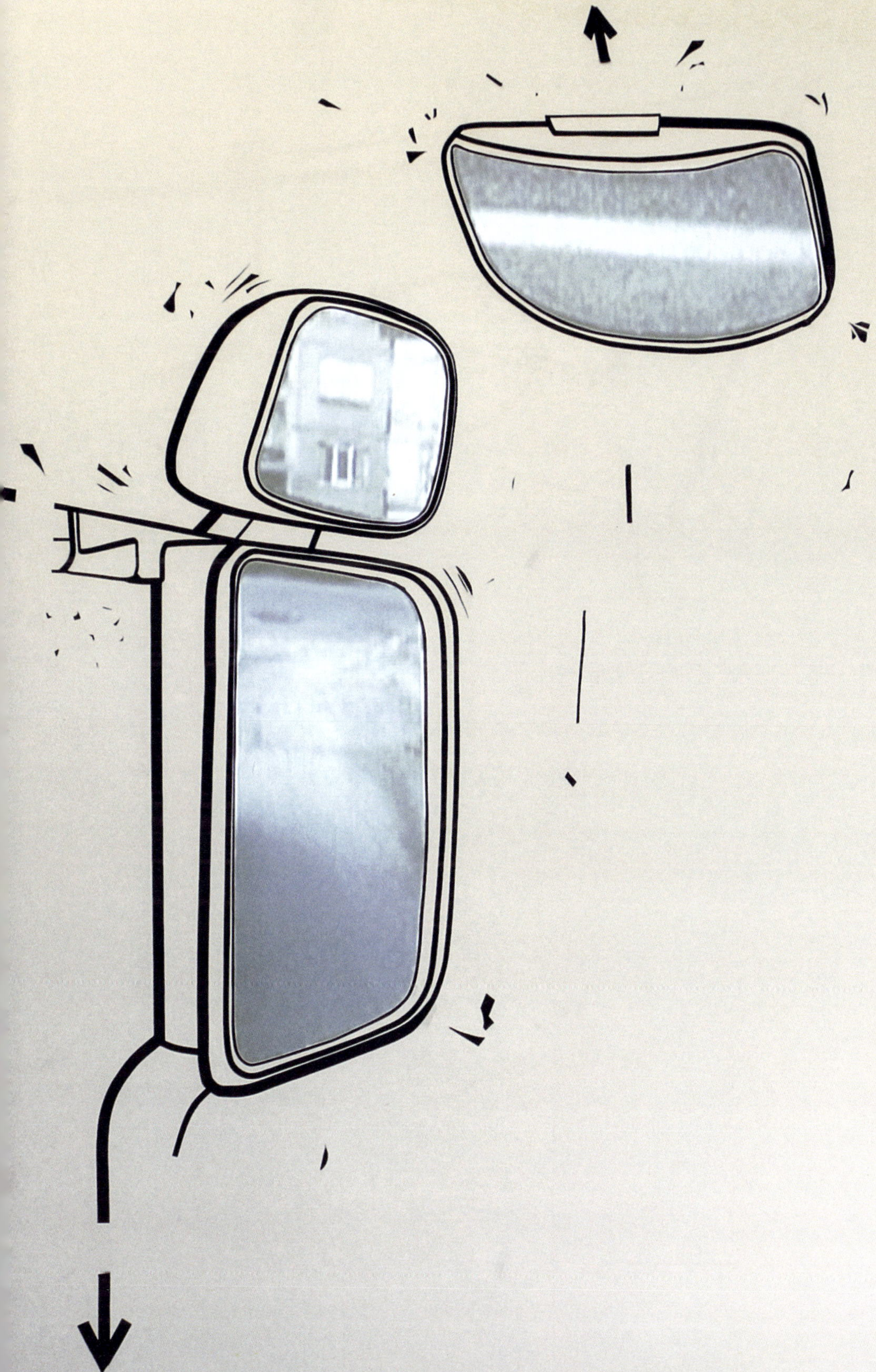

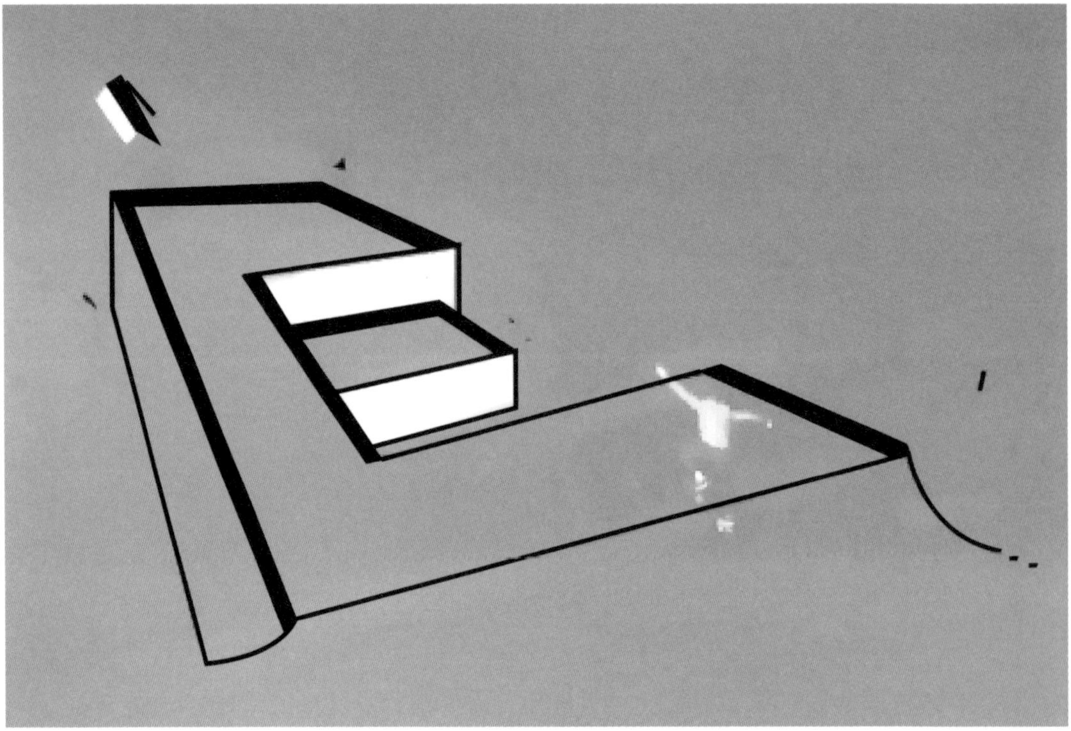

E
Insulating tape and video projection
Variable measurements
2011

>
1
Insulating tape and
video projection
Variable measurements
2011

>
2
Ink and video projection
Variable measurements
2011

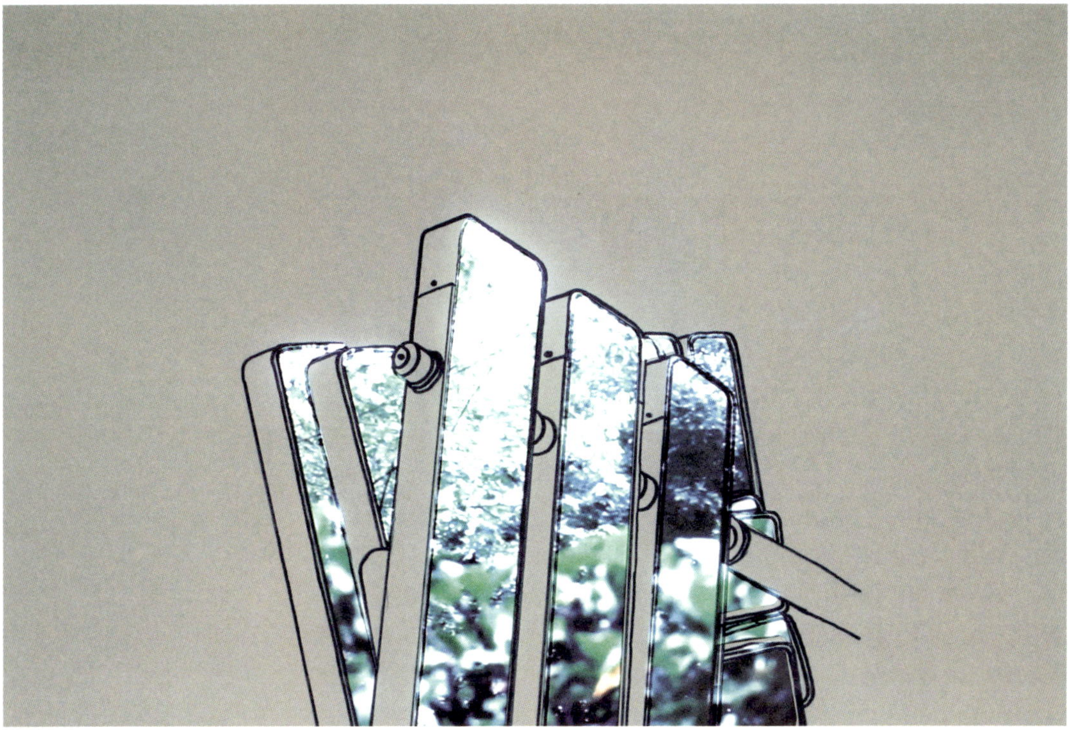

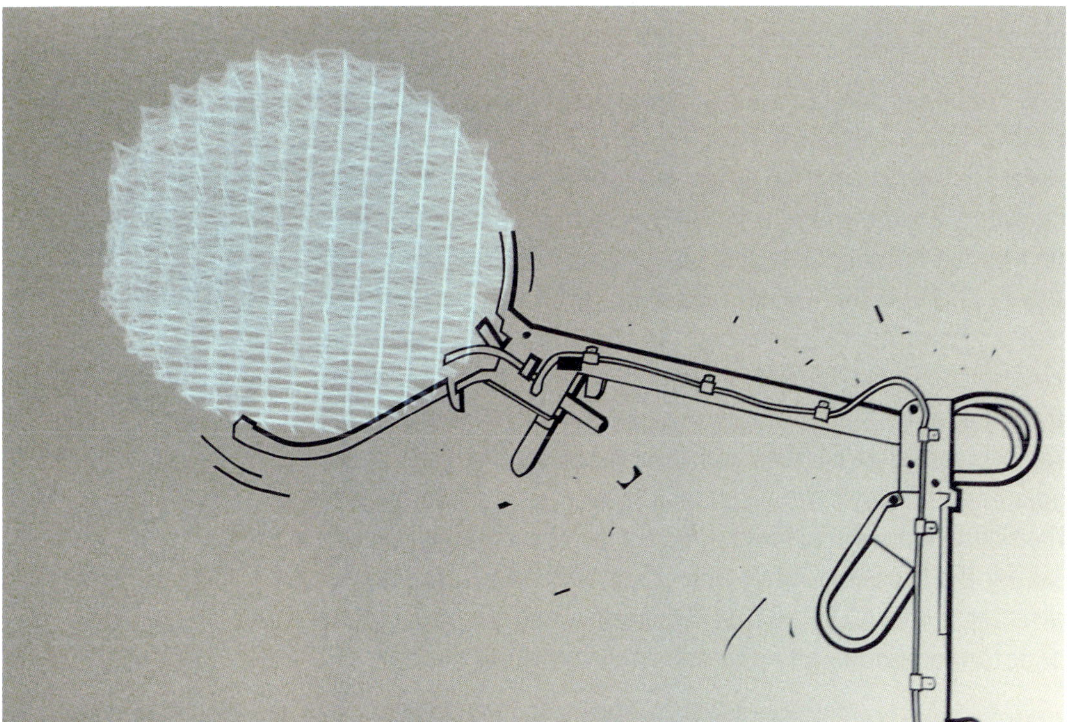

Francesc Ruiz

Through drawings with unfinished storylines, Francesc Ruiz creates credible representations of forms of social urbanism, translated into standardised forms of conduct that societies have developed or tend to develop in the numerous spaces of public coexistence that the city generates, both in real life and in the imaginary iconography of the world of print. With these drawings, which he often converts into mural pieces on a monumental scale, he weaves stories that are possible, fictionalised, treated with black humour, that eventually allow a glimpse of conflicts that we can find in any construction of urban collectivity.

The Funhouse is an installation that simulates a hall of distorting mirrors similar to those that we find in funfairs. Unfolding in its interior is an ambiguous representation of characters undergoing a collective catharsis, which would be like the reflections of the spectators in the exhibition hall itself. Through this artistic drawing, digitally manipulated and augmented to a life-size scale, the artist places us before an existential space jammed with a series of uncontrolled actions by the protagonists trapped inside a parodic reverberation of mirrors that accentuates the drift of the scene. In this work the artist makes an implicit reference to the behavioural receptivity at the heart of contemporary art, taking the museum itself into a state of alienation where director, visitors and all that it contains, charge into a game of deformed languages and deceitful realities.

The installation *Les portes (Lleida)* proposes another form of urban meta-narrative. Through a very broad archive of photographs of facades of buildings in Lleida, the artist makes up covers of publications that work like small architectures by permitting access to the same number of interiors of houses in the same city, through images taken from property sales and rental websites. Francesc Ruíz transfers, thus, the spectator to a handmade maquette of the city that each can visit and manage, creating their own route, putting into practice a kind of random voyeurism through the interior of hundreds of home scenarios that show the close (and simultaneously inevitable) particularities that arise in a single collectivity to which they belong. An apparently casual act, like someone browsing a record or comics shop and thumbing through the contents, or, in this case, the remains of a vulnerable property market pushed with impunity into a nosedive by the recent economic and speculative situation. These private spaces in the city, self-exhibited in a fragile fashion, are disturbing because of the signs they incorporate of a growing phenomenon of public depredation.

Teresa Blanch

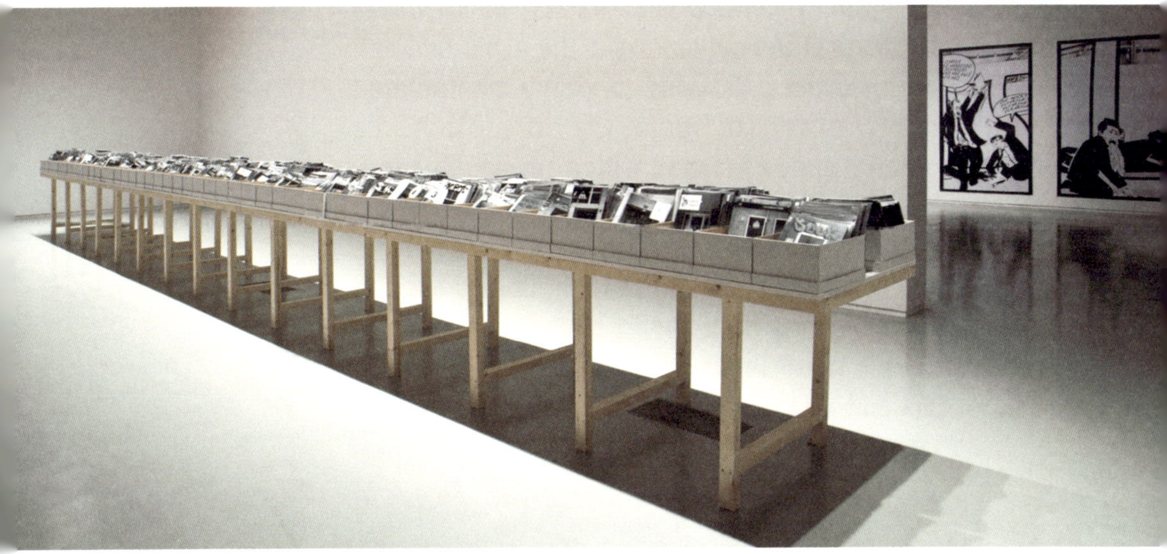

Les portes (Lleida)

6,000 digitally printed magazines, boxes,
2 tables measuring 77 x 85 x 235 cm each
2009

Les portes (Lleida) is formed by around 6,000 magazines that are organised along an 11-metre table that is reminiscent of the displays that we usually find in shops selling comics. The installation is like a folded maquette of the city of Lleida in which, starting with the basic structure of a publication, the covers have been substituted by doors, the titles by different graphic elements existing on the streets of Lleida and the interiors by photographs of homes in the city extracted from what I call tangential cyber-geographic tools, such as websites for the sale and rental of apartments.

When confronted with the work, the spectator finds himself before a new version of the city in which the linear nature of the urban tour is interrupted, allowing him to jump from one place in the city to another easily, to move from one door to another and penetrate them to find out what the interiors of homes in Lleida look like and how they are modelled by their inhabitants.

The piece also makes reference to the current situation of the Spanish economic system and the crisis in the property sector, and under this viewpoint the piece seems to be a kind of market of property bargains in which the owners have been substituted by banks, building societies, insurance companies and institutions of all kinds, and this is set against some transgressive elements of the urban landscape such as graffiti or agitprop posters, which only serve to underline who owns the city and who owns its citizens.

Francesc Ruiz

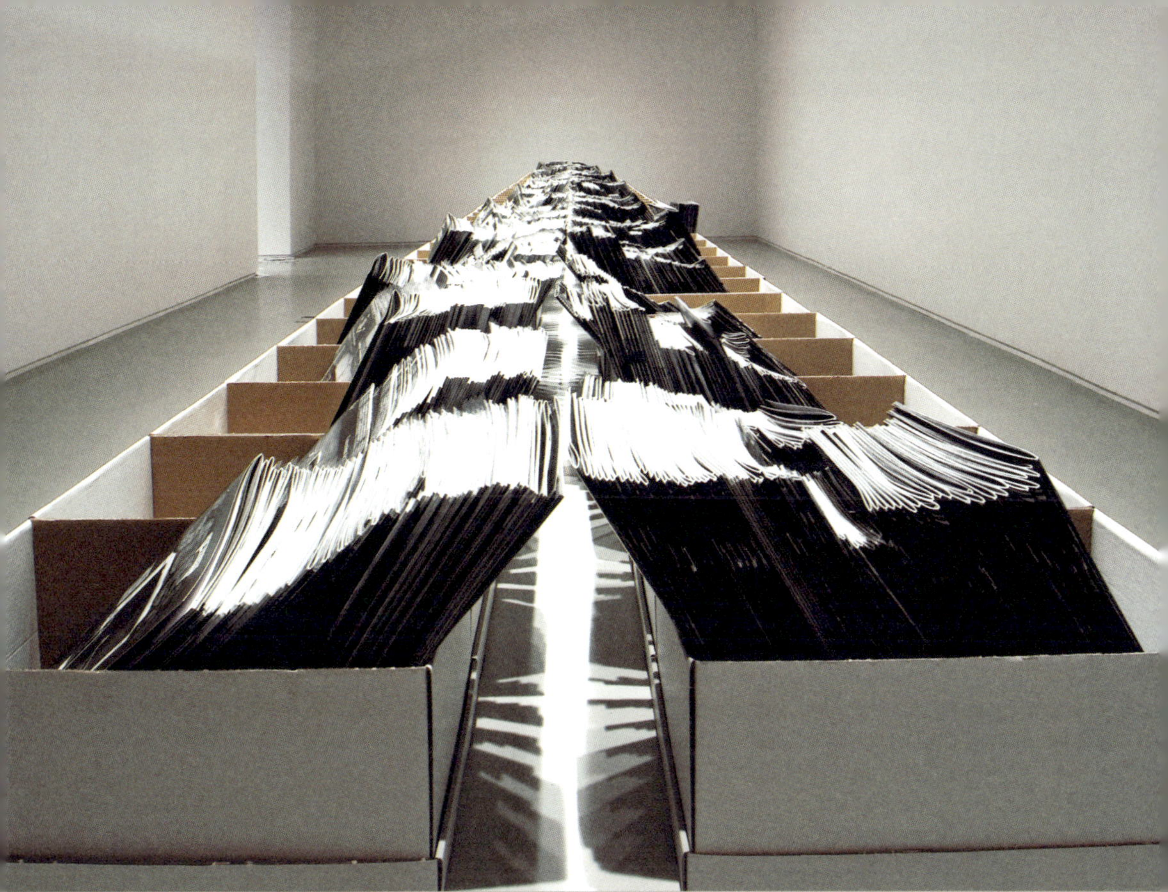

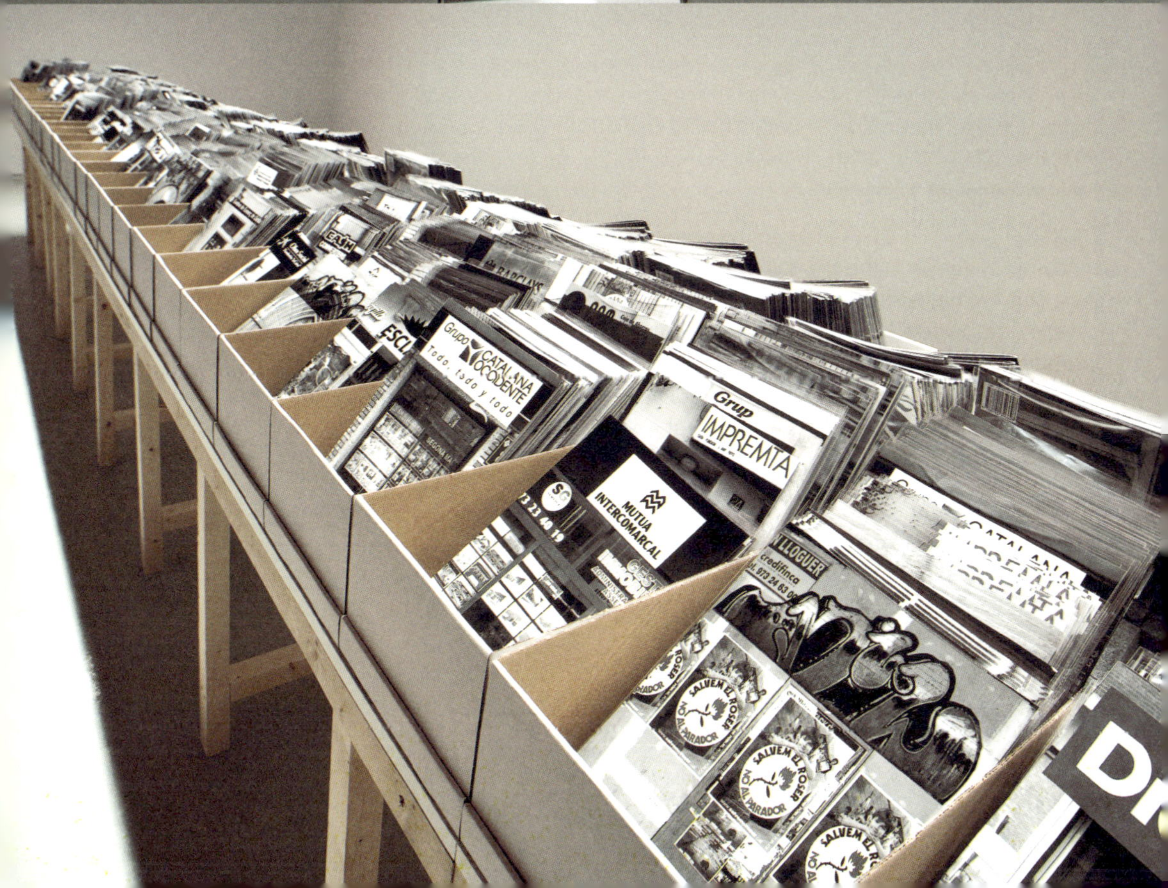

Grupo CATALANA OCCIDENTE
Todo, todo y todo
Grup IMPREMTA
MUTUA INTERCOMARCAL
LLOGUER
SALVEM EL ROSER
NO AL PARADOR

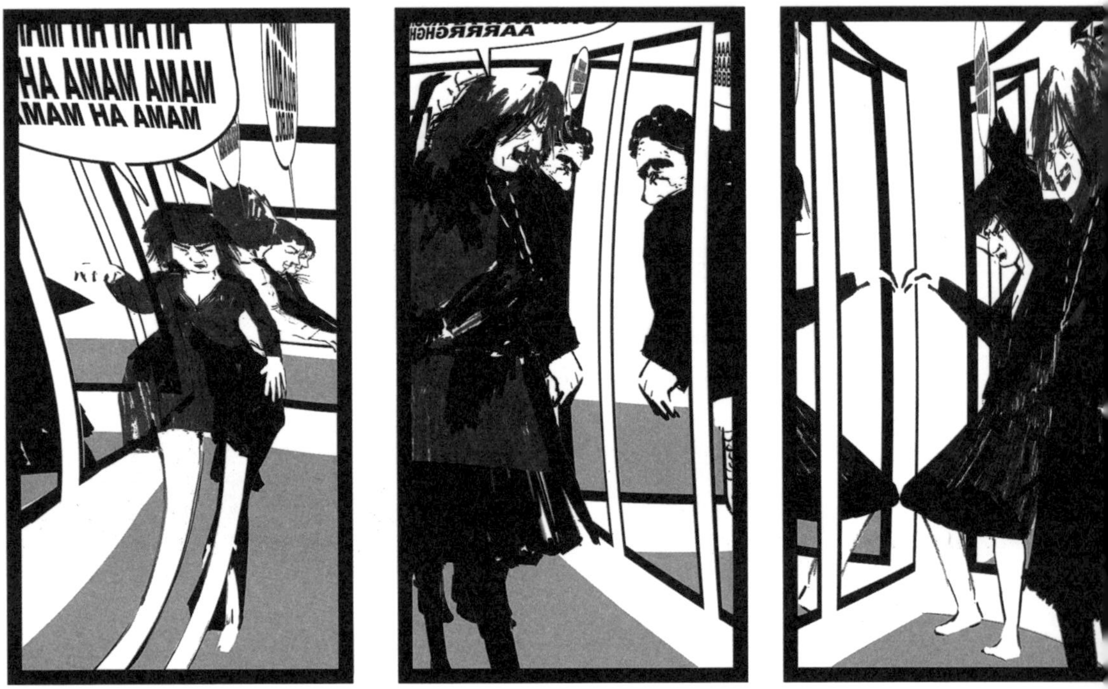

The_Funhouse
5 panels, digital print on Forex 10 mm
130 x 230 cm
2011

The Funhouse is a series of site-specific installations that take on a new form every time they are exhibited. I like to think of them as a system of representation that, through the use of some very basic elements from the language of the comic, creates a parallel world that entirely occupies the exhibition space.

The space is covered with large-sized cartoon strips that also take on the function of distorting mirrors, like those of the hall of mirrors at a funfair. These mirror-cartoons reflect each other creating a *mise en abîme* that shows a group of characters who seem to be taking part in a cathartic ritual. The characters express themselves through speech bubbles, that also react to the physics of the mirrors, with the text becoming inverted, and the language and writing deconstructed.

The work questions the place and the status of the spectator, revealing his repressed pathos, confronting him with an uncomfortable reality and with his role within the institution of art. In turn, the piece links comic and architecture in a tradition that relates it with the installations of mirrors by Pistoletto or the glass pavilions of Dan Graham.

Francesc Ruiz

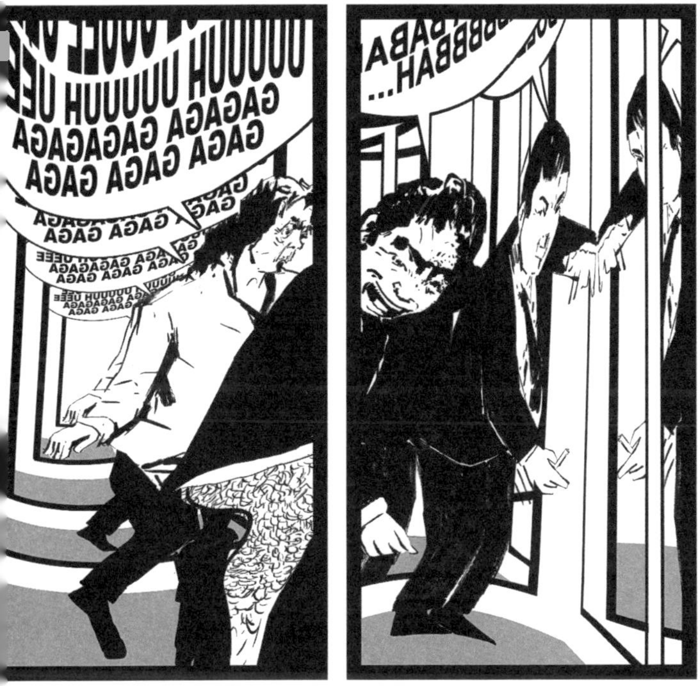

The meaning of reading

From there it follows that a fundamental characteristic of his work is generosity: excess as a way of breaking the circle of official readings, of breaking the chain of the discourse with possible associations that link the individual to a determined option. A political sense of the open account that constructs a liquid subjectivity, one which offers as many possibilities for subjection as subtexts, allowing the changing adoption of a relevancy and in turn of its contrary. Like in an open-minded citizen on an urban tour, the concentric nature of sub-cultural focuses is broken through their analogy, the alternative enjoyment of each of the options at his disposal: the same that the style of cultural tales about the Bible dismantle and reposition in their content over and again in an infinite exegesis. What is disturbing is that possibility that is interchangeable with another: his narrative delivers the assuaging possibility of diversity. That is where that political nature of his work lies: political from the moment that the individual is produced by the social order that organises and incites his experiences at a given time in history."

Manuel Segade
in Francesc Ruiz, *La visita guiada*, MNCARS, Madrid, 2008

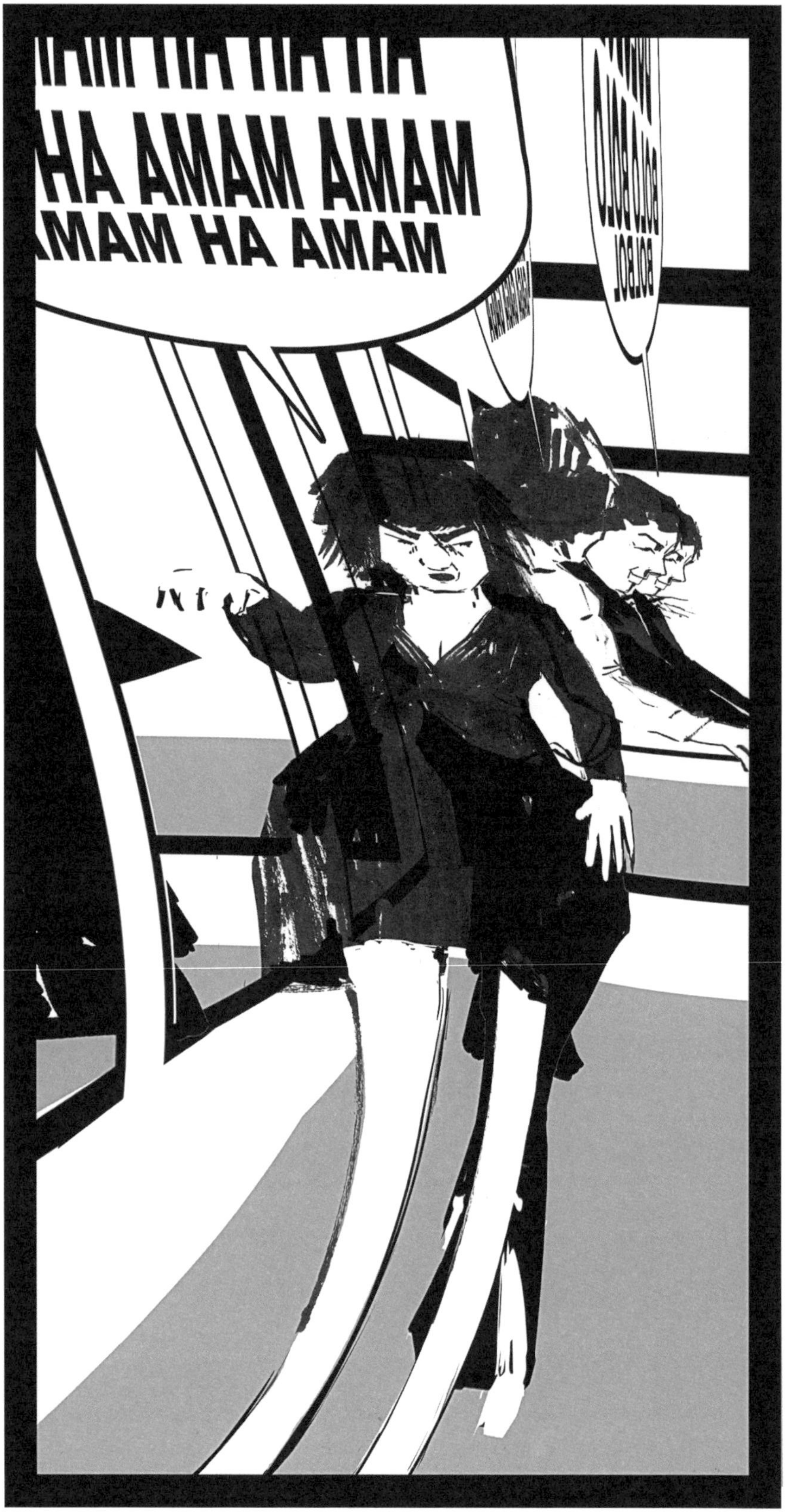
HA AMAM AMAM
AMAM HA AMAM

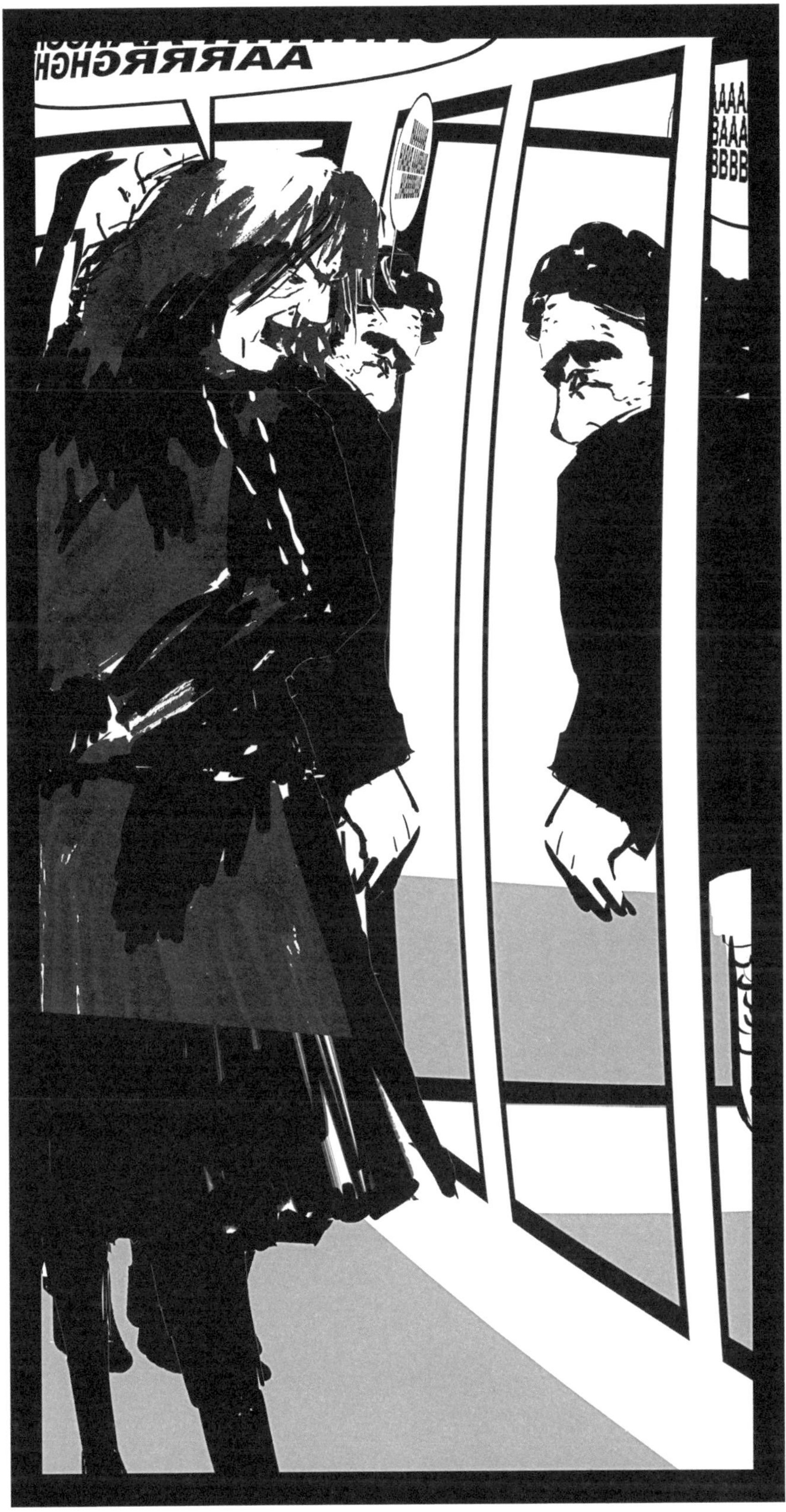
AARRGHGH

Mauro Cerqueira

Guimarães (Portugal), 1982. He lives and works in Porto (Portugal).

Selected solo exhibitions

2011 *Senhor dos Aflitos.* Centro de Artes Visuais, Coimbra (Portugal).
China. Antigo Posto dos Correios, Castelo Branco (Portugal).
Trepadeira nº1. Solo Project, Swab Art Fair, Barcelona (Spain).
2010 *Serin e as trepadeiras.* Laboratório das Artes, Guimarães (Portugal).
Michael. Galeria Gomes Alves, Guimarães (Portugal).
Looking the City. Threshold Artspace, Perth (United Kingdom).
Engoliu a espinha e foi operado para o poderem enforcar no dia seguinte. Curated by Adriano Pedrosa. Solo Projects. Arco, Madrid (Spain).
Jim. Galeria Graça Brandão, Lisbon (Portugal).
2009 *Como passos num chão oco e escavado por baixo.* Empty Cube, Galeria do Instituto Politécnico de Tomar (Portugal).
Sua boca, aberta para gritar, estava cheia de terra. Kunsthalle Lissabon, Lisbon (Portugal).
Falling from Grace. The Mews, London (United Kingdom).
Desenhos do Sol. Round the Corner, Lisbon (Portugal).
Lição nº 2. Espaço Campanhã, Porto (Portugal).
2008 *Derrapagem.* Galeria Reflexus, Porto (Portugal).
A Festa do Fim do Mundo. A Sala, Porto (Portugal).
Se morrer morri. Galeria Reflexus, Porto (Portugal).
2007 *Menos que zero.* Galeria Gomes Alves, Guimarães (Portugal).
Base. Atelier da ESAG, Guimarães (Portugal).
2006 *Wacky Races* (a dialogue with André Sousa). PêssegosPraSemana, Porto (Portugal).
Rocket Ship. Apêndice, Porto (Portugal).
Fuckers. Wasser-Bassin, Porto (Portugal).

Recent group exhibitions

2011 *Il Buen Vicino.* Curated by Alessandra Poggianti. Chiesa del Luogo Pio, Livorno (Italy).
An Urban Silent. The Exchange and Newlyn Art Gallery, Penzance (United Kingdom).
Oreja Naufragio (a dialogue with Julia Spínola). Galería Heinrich Ehrhardt, Madrid (Spain).
Sem pé (a dialogue with Nuno Sousa Vieira). Galeria Casa Triângulo, São Paulo (Brazil).
Pó esquerdo (a dialogue with Nuno Sousa Vieira). Galeria Nuno Centeno, Porto (Portugal).
Somewhere Else. Curated by Direlia Lazo. Galeria Nogueras Blanchard, Barcelona (Spain).
Art for Life / Art for Living. Swab Art Fair, Barcelona (Spain).
X Prémio União Latina. Centro Cultural de Cascais (Portugal).
O Museu em ruínas. Museu de Arte Contemporânea de Elvas (Portugal).
Ceci n'est pas une rétrospective - In. Tranzit + W.C. Container. Padaria Independente, Porto (Portugal).
2010 *A culpa não é minha.* Museu Colecção Berardo, Lisbon (Portugal).

Pepe Cifuentes

Pepe Cifuentes was born in Seville (Spain) in 1975, and from an early age he showed a keen interest in TV, shunning children's games and other distractions. When at the age of five he saw his first film in a cinema, he stopped saying that he wanted to be a priest when he grew up and insisted for a long time that he wanted to make films, showing signs of a healthy ambition for orchestrating large-scale rituals. At his first communion he ignored the rest of his presents and concentrated on a small Werlisa still camera to produce his first and premonitory audiovisual work, *My First Communion*, which was praised at his Salesian school. For his eleventh birthday he was given a CineExín projector, with which for years he showed over and over again the four films he had. In the summer of 1989 the first domestic video camera entered the house, and a few months later Pepe filmed the fall of the Berlin Wall from the TV screen, showing a growing interest in documenting events of historical importance. During the last twenty years Pepe has devoted himself to his company, Cifuentes BBC TV, with which he gives audiovisual coverage to various celebrations and rituals. In all this time he has never ceased to watch television and download films from Internet to hone his directing skills.

Among Pepe Cifuentes' domestic works that have enjoyed the widest recognition, we have to single out *Esperanza Mora Rato, 101 años y todavía dirige la matanza* (In Memoriam), MiniDVPro, 45' (2006); *Marisa y Luisiño aún se tratan con cariño. Sus bodas de plata,* MiniDVPro, 29' (2003) and *Caricias, piropos y álbum de fotos,* MiniDVPro, 28' (2001).

Patricia Dauder

Barcelona (Spain), 1973. She lives and works in Barcelona.

Solo exhibitions

2012 *Studio nº 3. Patricia Dauder.* Galerie Van der Mieden, Antwerpen (Belgium).
2011 *Modular.* Aanant & Zoo, Berlin (Germany).
2010 *Forward (slides).* Navio Vazio, Porto (Portugal).
Teahupoo. Galeria ProjecteSD, Barcelona (Spain).
2009 *Art Statement.* Art Basel, Basel (Switzerland).
Fundació Suñol, Barcelona (Spain).
2008 *Les Maliens (A script + A film).* Museu de l'Empordà, Figueres (Spain).
2007 *Patricia Dauder.* Galeria ProjecteSD, Barcelona (Spain).
2006 *Les Maliens (a script).* Black Box, Arco 2006, Galeria ProjecteSD, Barcelona (Spain).
2005 *Pel·lícula Abstracta I i altres dibuixos.* Galeria ProjecteSD, Barcelona (Spain).
2003 *M.* Galeria ProjecteSD, Barcelona (Spain).
Interferències 03. Curated by Manel Clot. Casa Soler i Palet, Terrassa (Spain).
Instal·lació 0.2. Galeria Antonio de Barnola, Barcelona (Spain).
Those whom we don't see. Galeria Antonio de Barnola, Barcelona (Spain).
1998 Sala Fortuny, Centre de lectura de Reus (Spain).
Subjects Focusing. Artis S'Hertogenbosch (Netherlands).

Recent group exhibitions

2012 *Object Fictions.* James Cohan Gallery, New York (United States).
2011 *Test Transmission.* Artspace, Auckland (New Zeland).
Even in the quietest moments. Vogt Gallery, New York (United States).
1979. Un monument a instants radicals. La Virreina, Centre de la imatge, Barcelona (Spain).
2010 *Patricia Dauder, Dani Gal.* Galerie Kadel Willborn, Karlsruhe (Germany).
Nosotras. Centro Andaluz de Arte Contemporáneo, Seville (Spain).
2009 *Été 2009.* Galerie Jocelyn Wolff, Paris (France).
There is No(w) Romanticism. Galerie Les Filles du Calvaire, Brussels (Belgium).
Los tiempos de un lugar. Curated by Neus Miró. CDAN (Fundación Beulas), Huesca (Spain).
2008 *Lugares Comprometidos: Topografía y Actualidad.* Fundación ICO, PHE 08, Madrid (Spain). Curated by Sérgio Mah.
Prospect 58. Antwerpen (Belgium).
Itinerarios 06-07. XIV Becas de Artes Plásticas, Fundación Marcelino Botín, Santander (Spain).
2007 III Bienal de Jafre (Spain).
Keine Zeichnung, Keine Zeichner. Kunstverein Rügen (Germany).
Cosas Humanas. Impex, Budapest (Hungary).
2006 *Generación 2006.* La Casa Encendida, Madrid and La Capella, Barcelona (Spain).
Historias Diferidas. Obra Social Caja Madrid, Sala Alcalá 31, Madrid (Spain).
Alguns llibres d'artista (A few artist's books). Galeria ProjecteSD, Barcelona (Spain).

Carla Filipe

Vila Nova da Barquinha (Portugal), 1973. She lives and works in Porto (Portugal).

Selected solo exhibitions

2011 *Bordas de Alguidar.* Galeria Graça Brandão, Lisbon (Portugal).
Experiência Flutuante - Paisagens Gráficas. Galeria Nuno Centeno, Porto (Portugal).
Arquivo Surdo-Mudo / Deaf and Dumb Archive. Tranzit Display, Prague (Czech Republic).
Saloio. Estufa da Tapada das Necessidades, Lisbon (Portugal).
2010 *O Povo reunido jamais será - Representações gráficas.* Museu do Neo-Realismo, Vila Franca de Xira (Portugal).
É um espaço estranho e maravilhoso, o ar é seco, quente e insípido - Precarious, Escape, Fascination. Kunsthalle Lissabon, Lisbon (Portugal).
2009 *Quem espera é pobre.* Galeria Reflexus, Porto (Portugal).
Estas coisas levam tempo. Espaço Campanhã, Porto (Portugal).
2007 *Desertar.* InTransit, Porto (Portugal).
Obrigado pela conversa . A Sala, Porto (Portugal).
2005 *Without Name.* Galeria Quadrado Azul, Porto (Portugal).
2004 *Zona de Estar.* Salão Olímpico, Porto (Portugal).

Recent group exhibitions

2011 *All to Wall (part II).* Galeria Cristina Guerra, Lisbon (Portugal).
V Bienal de Jafre (Spain).
Prémio EDP Novos Artistas. Museu da Electricidade, Lisbon (Portugal).
Transporto sempre uma viagem. Galeria Quadrum, Lisbon (Portugal).
2010 *Manifesta 8.* Curated by Tranzit. Murcia (Spain).
Arena. Fundação Carmona e Costa, Lisbon (Portugal).
Ceci n`est pas une rétrospective. Padaria Independente, Porto (Portugal).
2009 *Entroncamento.* Espaço Avenida, Lisbon (Portugal).
Hospitalidade. Hospital de São João, Porto (Portugal).
Está a morrer e não quer ver. Espaço Campanhã, Porto (Portugal).
2008 *Part-ilha.* Spike Island, Bristol (United Kingdom).
2007 *INTRO.* Contretype, Brussels (Bélgica).
Antimonumentos. Galeria António Henriques, Viseu (Portugal).
Pack. Edifício da Reitoria da Universidade do Porto (Portugal).
2006 *Busca Pólos.* Centro Cultural Vila Flor, Guimarães (Portugal).
Busca Pólos. Pavilhão de Portugal, Coimbra, co-produced with Museu de Arte Contemporânea de Serralves, Porto (Portugal).
2005 *Tóxic- O Discurso do Excesso.* Terminal e Plano 21, Oeiras (Portugal).
Desenhar o Discurso - Digressões sobre uma urbanidade disruptiva. Vila Nova de Cerveira (Portugal).
2004 *O Homem Invisível.* ZDB, Lisbon (Portugal).
Salão Olímpico, Artecontempo, Lisbon (Portugal).

Nuria Fuster

Alcoi (Spain), 1978. She lives and works in Madrid (Spain).

Selected solo exhibitions

2011 Explum. Puerto Lumbreras, Murcia (Spain).
2009 *Camino Subterráneo / Subterranean Way.* Galería Marta Cervera, Madrid (Spain).
2008 *Structural Events.* Hamish Morrison Galerie, Berlin (Germany).
2007 *Arquitecturas domésticas.* Galería Marta Cervera, Madrid (Spain).
2004 Galeria Metropolitana Barcelona, Barcelona (Spain).

Recent group exhibitions

2012 Marike Schuurman & Nuria Fuster. Hamish Morrison Galerie, Berlin (Germany).
Generaciones 2012. La Casa Encendida, Madrid (Spain).
2011 *Sin Título, 2011. Técnica Mixta, medidas variables.* Espacio Gran Vía, Madrid (Spain).
Hambre, 3ª edición. Madrid (Spain).
Biblioteca intervenida. Espacio F, Madrid (Spain).
Arco 2011. Galería Marta Cervera, Madrid (Spain).
Cruce de relatos. CADA, Alcoi (Spain).
2010 NADA. Miami Art Fair. Galería Marta Cervera, Miami (United States).
Antes que todo. CA2M, Móstoles (Spain).
25 Años de la Muestra de Arte Injuve. Círculo de Bellas Artes, Madrid (Spain).
PhotoEspaña 2010. Galería Marta Cervera, Madrid (Spain).
Itinerarios 08/09. Fundación Botín, Santander (Spain).
Arco 2010. Galería Marta Cervera, Madrid (Spain).
Cartografías de la Creatividad: 100% Valencianos. Centre del Carme, València (Spain) and Museo de Arte.
Contemporáneo de Santo Domingo (Dominican Republic).
EspacioAtlántico, Feria de arte contemporáneo. Galería Marta Cervera, Vigo (Spain).
Fundación Palma Espacios de Arte. Casal Solleric, Mallorca (Spain).
Explum'10. Certamen Internacional Arte Actual, Murcia (Spain).
2009 NADA. Galería Marta Cervera, Miami (United States).
Antes de ayer y pasado mañana; o lo que puede ser pintura hoy. MACUF, A Coruña (Spain).
La vida en este lado. Galería Espacio Líquido, Gijón (Spain).
Enlaces+4. Últimas adquisiciones de la Colección Arte Contemporáneo. Patio Herreriano, Valladolid (Spain).
MadridFoto. Galería Marta Cervera. Madrid (Spain).
Arco'09. Galería Marta Cervera, Madrid (Spain).
Nuria Fuster, Begoña Goyenetxea, Chris Johanson, Lara Schnitger, Katherine Bernhardt. Galería Marta Cervera, Madrid (Spain).
Muestra de artes visuales Injuve. Centro cultural Parque de España, Rosario (Argentina).
Hambre 09. Espacio Atocha24, Madrid (Spain).
Explum. Certamen Internacional Arte Actual. Colectivo Lobak. Puerto Lumbreras, Murcia (Spain).

Santiago Giralda

Madrid (Spain), 1980. Academic studies in Hamburg and Madrid, where he lives at present.

Solo exhibitions

2009 *Interior / Exterior.* Centro de Arte Joven, Comunidad de Madrid (Spain).
Under construction. Galería Punto, Valencia (Spain).
2007 *Outsider.* Ol-fru h Galerie, Hamburg (Germany).

Recent group exhibitions

2011 V Certamen de Pintura «Acisclo Antonio Palomino». SAFA, Bujalance, Córdoba (Spain).
Escala 1:1. Centro de Arte Matadero, Madrid (Spain).
X Certamen Virgen de las Viñas. Museo de Arte Contemporáneo Infanta Elena, Tomelloso (Spain).
2010 Tentaciones, Feria de la Estampación y Arte Múltiple Estampa, Madrid (Spain).
25 Años de la Muestra de Arte Injuve. Círculo de Bellas Artes, Madrid (Spain).
Artesantander, Feria de Arte Contemporáneo. Galería Mito, Santander (Spain).
Premio de Pintura Focus-Abengoa. Fundación Focus-Abengoa, Seville (Spain).
Exposición fin de máster. Facultad de Bellas Artes, Universidad Complutense de Madrid (Spain).
Swab, International Contemporary Art Fair. Galería Mito, Barcelona (Spain).
Forosur, Feria Iberoamericana de Arte Contemporáneo. Galería Mito, Cáceres (Spain).
New Realisms. Galería Mito, Barcelona (Spain).
2009 XXXVI Premio Bancaja de Pintura y Escultura. IVAM, Valencia (Spain).
70 Exposición Internacional de Artes Plásticas. Museo Municipal, Valdepeñas (Spain).
Program Preview. Galería Punto, Valencia (Spain).
2008 Muestra de Artes Visuales Injuve. Madrid and León (Spain).
Guatemala Cuty (Guatemala) and Santo Domingo (Dominican Republic).
Generaciones 2008. Cajamadrid, Madrid, Barcelona, Valencia and Seville (Spain).
Uno más es multitud, Doméstico 08. Curated by Tania Pardo. Madrid (Spain).
2007 *Fernweh / Heimweh.* Aol Gebaude, Hamburg (Germany).
XI Premio Carriegos de Pintura. La Casona, León (Spain).
XXVIII Certamen de Pintura Gredos. Casa de la Cultura, Arenas de San Pedro (Spain).
XXVII Certamen de Pintura «Ciudad de Manzanares», Pabellón de la Cultura, Manzanares (Spain).
Certamen de Pintura Uned. Institut français, Madrid (Spain).
2006 *Casa demolida.* Haubachstrasse 7a, Hamburg (Germany).
Jahresausstellung. Hochschule für Bildende Künste, Hamburg (Germany).
XXI Certamen de pintura BMW. Travelling exhibition, Madrid and Oviedo (Spain).

Jaime_de_la_Jara

Madrid (Spain), 1972.

Solo exhibitions

2011 *Tid project.* Hambre, Madrid (Spain).
2010 *The Navel.* Galería Fúcares, Madrid (Spain).
2009 *Lie.* Centre d'Art Tecla Sala, L'Hospitalet de Llobregat (Spain).
Curtain 3_ Poe Solution. Museo de Arte Contemporáneo español, Patio Herreriano, Valladolid (Spain).
2008 *Laying.* Cubo Azul, León (Spain).
2007 *15 inches.* Galería Fúcares, Madrid (Spain).
2005 *Big-Suite.* Galería Fúcares, Almagro (Spain).
2004 Galeria Palma 12, Vilafranca del Penedès (Spain).
Reflect on. Solo project, Loop, Barcelona (Spain).
2003 Sala de Arte Joven de la Comunidad de Madrid (Spain).

Group exhibitions

2011 *La Colección.* Museo de Arte Contemporáneo español Patio Herreriano, Valladolid (Spain).
N'Casa. Galería Fúcares, Almagro (Spain).
Celdas. Opening show at Centro de Arte La Cárcel de Segovia (Spain).
Sin título, técnica mixta, medidas variables. Gran Vía 67, Madrid (Spain).
Cómplices de futuro. Fundación Coca-Cola, Centro de Arte Alcobendas, Madrid (Spain).
2010 *Les Rencontres internationales.* Museo Nacional Centro de Arte Reina Sofía, Madrid (Spain).
Colección Coca-Cola, Da2, Salamanca (Spain).
Les Rencontres internationales. Archistruktur, Haus der Kulturen, Berlin (Germany).
2009 *Les Rencontres internationales*, Centre Pompidou, Paris (France).
El tiempo que venga - La Colección IX. Museo Artium de Vitoria-Gasteiz (Spain).
Artorama. Marseille (France).
Fotografías que ver en Madrid antes de estar muerto. Galería Fúcares, Madrid (Spain).
Nuevas adquisiciones de la Colección del Museo Patio Herreriano, Valladolid (Spain).
2008 Opening show at Fundación Iberia. Beijing (China).
Topografías urbanas. Galería Fúcares, Almagro (Spain).
2007 *Destino futuro.* Jardín Botánico, Madrid (Spain).
Planes futuros. Centro Baluarte, Pamplona (Spain).
2006 Generaciones 2006. Santa Inés, Seville; La Capella, Barcelona; Mercado del Este, Santander; La Casa Encendida, Madrid (Spain).
20 años de la Colección. Ayuntamiento de Pamplona (Spain).
Casal de Solleric. Premi Ciutat de Palma, Mallorca (Spain).
Art-TV. Centro Andaluz de Arte Contemporáneo, Málaga (Spain).
2005 V Bienal de Artes Plásticas Rafael Botí, Córdoba (Spain).
Bienal de Pamplona. La Ciudadela, Pamplona (Spain).
Generaciones 2005. Espai Caja Madrid, Barcelona; Mercado del Este, Santander; La Casa Encendida, Madrid (Spain).
Reflect_on(fly) Solo project, Loop, Barcelona (Spain).
El Barco del Arte, Bilbao (Spain).

Miki_Leal

Seville (Spain), 1974.

Solo exhibitions

2010 *Il Cellesse.* Galería Fúcares, Madrid (Spain).
La Cabaña / De la Costa Azul a la Selva Negra. Becas de Artes Visuales Cajasol 2010. Centro Cultural Cajasol, Espacio Escala y Sala Imagen, Seville; Hospedería Fonseca, Salamanca (Spain).
2009 *Mikithology.* Galería Fúcares, Almagro (Spain).
Trasfábula (with Abraham Lacalle and MP & MP Rosado). Sala de exposiciones Hospedería Fonseca, Universidad de Salamanca (Spain).
The end. Benveniste Contemporary, Madrid (Spain).
2008 *Ieri, oggi, domani.* Galería Alessandro Seno, Milano (Italy).
Con el viento de cara. Galería Rafael Ortiz, Seville (Spain).
Frenhofer y La Laguna. Galería Maribel López, Berlin (Germany).
2007 *Balada Heavy.* Galería Magda Bellotti, Madrid; Galería Milagros Delicado, Cádiz (Spain).
2006 *El estudio del pintor.* Galería Paolo Maria Deanesi, Rovereto (Italy).
2005 *El manantial, el nadador y la pintura.* Galería Magda Bellotti, Madrid (Spain).
2003 *Canadalia.* Galería Magda Bellotti, Madrid (Spain).
Mikithology. Galería Cavecanem, Seville (Spain).
2001 *Patrulla RCH 2001,* a Richard Channin Foundation Project for Galería Cavecanem, Seville (Spain).
2000 *Proyecto para un oasis.* Galería Isabel Ignacio, Seville (Spain).

Recent group exhibitions

2012 *Lejos de casa.* Curated by Virginia Torrente. Galeria Mas Art, Barcelona (Spain).
2011 *El puente de la visión.* Museo de Arte Contemporáneo de Santander y Cantabria, Santander (Spain).
Colección de pintura contemporánea internacional. Fundación Barrié, Sede A Coruña (Spain).
Miki Leal & Abraham Lacalle. Baldini Baker: The Spanish Syndicate. Curated by Kevin Power. Track 16 Gallery, Santa Monica (United States).
S/T. Gran Vía 67, Madrid (Spain).
2010 *Sevilla, ozú, qué caló!* Curated by Jesús Reina Palazón. Galería Fúcares, Almagro (Spain).
La imagen y el animal. Curated by Javier Sánchez. Sala de exposiciones del Palacio de los Condes de Gabia, Granada (Spain).
2009 *El tiempo que venga. La colección IX.* Curated by Daniel Castillejo. Artium, Vitoria-Gasteiz (Spain).
Auto. Sueño y materia. La cultura del automóvil como territorio crítico y creativo. Curated by Alberto Martín. LaBoral Centro de Arte y Creación Industrial, Gijón; CA2M, Móstoles (Spain).
2008 *Imágenes latentes.* Curated by Alberto Martín. Galería Fúcares, Madrid (Spain).
2006 *Planes futuros.* Baluarte, Pamplona (Spain).
Imágenes de la pintura. El pintor en su estudio. Museo de Cádiz (Spain).

Juan_López

Alto Maliaño (Spain), 1979.

Solo exhibitions

2011 *1812_2012. Una Mirada Contemporánea.* Artium, Vitoria-Gasteiz (Spain).
CARLOS. Desvelarte Festival, Santander (Spain).
Tokyo Story 2010, Aoyama. TWS, Tokyo (Japan).
The LOOP Fair. Galería La Fábrica, Barcelona (Spain).
2010 *Looking for patrons.* Archimobile of Matadero, Carpe Diem Arte e Pesquisa, Lisbon (Portugal).
2009 *Nevera.* The Black Pillar, Madrid (Spain).
New Grecas. Galería Valle Ortí. Valencia (Spain).
It's Tricky. Festival MEM. Apetit Gallery, Bilbao (Spain).
Galeria Nogueras-Blanchard, Barcelona (Spain).
Retrovisores. Bellevue, Linz (Austria).
Juan López. Sala Naos, Santander (Spain).
Arco 09. Solo Project. A collaboration with Galería La Fábrica, Madrid (Spain).
2008 *Hoy no aspiro a nada.* Espai 13, Fundació Joan Miró, Barcelona, Galería La Fábrica, Madrid (Spain).
2007 *Spider Lab.* Art intervention at LaBoral Centro de Arte y Creación Industrial, Gijón (Spain).
2006 Galería La Fábrica, Madrid (Spain).
2005 Juan López with PH Collection. Sala Mercado, Barcelona (Spain).
Para tu tara. Centre d'Art Santa Mònica, Barcelona (Spain).
Estuve en Toledo y me acordé de ti. Espacio Contemporáneo Archivo de Toledo (Spain).
2004 *One'n'One. Proyecto En Casa.* La Casa Encendida, Madrid (Spain).
www.perfornika.com. Works in the web.
2003 *Presentacion de «redibujo.02».* Museo de Bellas Artes de Santander (Spain).
www.joystick.org. Works in the web.
2002 *1 pone y Dios dispone.* Facultad de Bellas Artes de Cuenca (Spain).
2001 *Cube.* Galería Engler & Piper, Berlin (Germany).
2000 Exhibition at «La Casa». Tiradores Bajos F nº 47, Cuenca (Spain).
1999 Pub Minimal. Maliañoc(Spain).

Recent group exhibitions

2011 Impakt festival 2011: Urban Screen. Neude Square, Utrecht (Netherlands).
Aventuras de Líneas. Galería Eva Ruíz, Madrid (Spain).
Biblioteca Intervenida. Museo de Arte Moderno y Contemporáneo de Santander; Ingràvid Festival, Figueres; Espacio F, Madrid (Spain).
NEXT – TWS 10 Years!. TWS Shibuya, Tokyo (Japan).
We Like Santander. Foconorte, Santanderc(Spain).
Saltar de la página. De Velázquez a Canogar, 20 años de ABC Cultural. Museo ABC, Madrid (Spain).
Noche de Luna Llena. Segovia (Spain).
Diez años de fotografia española. Colección Coca-Cola. Instituto Cervantes of São Paulo, Rio de Janeiro, Brasilia and Salvador de Bahía (Brazil).
Cántabros en la Colección Norte. Biblioteca Central de Cantabria, Santander(Spain).
Open Studio. TWS, Tokyo (Japan).

Francesc_Ruiz

Barcelona (Spain), 1971. Lives and works in Barcelona.

Selected solo exhibitions

2011 *The Yaois.* Galeria Estrany-de la Mota, Barcelona (Spain).
The Paper Trail. Fundació Suñol, Barcelona (Spain).
100 i +. EtHall, Barcelona (Spain).
2010 *Gasworks Yaoi.* Gasworks, London (United Kingdom).
The Paper Trail. Contemporary Image Collective, Cairo (Egypt).
Sukia. White Cubicle at George and the Dragon, London (United Kingdom).
Instant Newsstand. Creative Time, New York (United States).
2009 *Big Boom.* Centre d'Art la Panera, Lleida (Spain).
2008 *Bcn Eye Trip.* Galeria Estrany-de la Mota. Barcelona (Spain).
La visita guiada / The Guided Tour. MNCARS, Monasterio de Santo Domingo de Silos (Spain).
Comic Brick. L'Estruch, Sabadell (Spain).
2007 *Game over expanded.* Maribel López Gallery, Berlin (Germany).
2006 *Kiosk Downtown.* Centre d'Art Santa Mònica, Barcelona (Spain).
La cosa. Periódico en cuarentena. Fundación Luis Seoane, A Coruña (Spain).

Recent group exhibitions

2011 *La qüestió del paradigma.* Centre d'Art La Panera, Lleida and La Capella, Barcelona (Spain).
Ficciones Urbanas. Koldo Mitxelena, San Sebastián (Spain).
Aproximaciones I. Fundación Helga de Alvear, Cáceres (Spain).
A las ciudades se las conoce como a las personas, al caminar. CAAC, Seville (Spain).
2010 *Antes que Todo.* CA2M, Móstoles (Spain).
The Graphic Unconscious. Philagrafika. Temple Gallery, Philadelphia (United States).
Medium Resistance. The Ice Box. Crane Arts. Philadelphia (United States).
Polirrubro. Francesc Ruiz, Fernando Llanos, Julio d'Angiolino. Centro Cultural de España, Buenos Aires (Argentina).
El mal d'escriptura. MACBA, Barcelona (Spain).
Biennale d'Art Contemporain. Le Havre (France).
Archi & BD - La ville dessinée. Cité de l'Architecture et du Patrimoine, Paris (France).
The Last Post. The Last Newspaper. New Museum, New York (United States).
2009 *Quizás me puedas contar otra historia...* Intervenciones Foro Sur, Cáceres (Spain).
Sequelism: Espisode 3: Possible, Probable or Preferable Futures. Arnolfini, Bristol (United Kingdom).
...Yo no tengo pesadillas, yo las genero. Oficina 26, Rosario (Argentina).
28th Biennial of Graphic Arts. Ljubljana Biennial of Arts. Ljubljana (Slovenia).
Territoris de Fricció. ACVIC, Centre d'arts contemporànies de Vic (Spain).
Methaphors of Un/Real. Animamix Biennial '09-'10, Shanghai (China).
The Pain Game. Nosbaum & Reding Art Contemporary, Luxemburg (Luxemburg).